# The Positive Coach Approach

## Call Center Coaching for High Performance

Sally Cordova and Judy McKee

Bloomington, IN  Milton Keynes, UK

*AuthorHouse™*
*1663 Liberty Drive, Suite 200*
*Bloomington, IN 47403*
*www.authorhouse.com*
*Phone: 1-800-839-8640*

*AuthorHouse™ UK Ltd.*
*500 Avebury Boulevard*
*Central Milton Keynes, MK9 2BE*
*www.authorhouse.co.uk*
*Phone: 08001974150*

*First published by AuthorHouse 2/1/2007*

*ISBN: 978-1-4259-7838-9 (sc)*

*Printed in the United States of America*
*Bloomington, Indiana*

*This book is printed on acid-free paper.*

*To Jim McKee, our mentor and coach. He taught us life lessons as well as management lessons during all of our lives together but most of all he believed in us with all his heart.*

# TABLE OF CONTENTS

# Chapter Six
## Foundational Imperative Three: Eight Guiding Principles 43

# Chapter Seven
## Learn To Listen 63

# Chapter Eight
## Foundational Imperative Four: High Five Method 69

# Chapter Nine
## Common Coaching Challenges 87

# Chapter One
# Introduction to
# Positive Coaching

Early in her training career, Judy McKee discovered that she, along with many other call center trainers, found trainees were interested and seemingly committed to adapting and using newly learned skills, techniques and attitudes. The trainees were "pumped up" full of fire, ready to take on the world, etc.

As part of Judy's usual mode, she made follow-up calls to centers a few days after training was completed to see how things were progressing. Sadly, in many cases she found that most of the trainees were slowly but surely slipping back into their old comfortable ways of handling calls. This situation was disappointing for the call center manager, and left supervisors and agents with unfulfilled expectations of increased performance.

After finding this "slippage" occurring much too often, Judy did some soul searching and closely examined the training process as carried on in most call centers. It didn't take long for her to isolate the "missing link" that she saw as the primary obstacle leading to the lack of long-term training success.

She realized that what undoubtedly contributes most to the "cooling down" phenomenon is the complete lack of ongoing positive coaching of the learned skills after the trainer has left the scene.

Judy's supposition is supported by statistics. Call centers where upper management support is strong, coupled with a structured positive coaching program, experience performance increases ranging from 20 to 90 percent, and agent turnover rates well below the call center norm.

Judy partially resolved this obstacle by including in her training programs a day of coaching. Both Judy's coaching style and method were very positive. When I joined McKee Motivation, I started out as a coach and used Judy's positive method.

Then, the most amazing thing happened. As I was coaching, managers and supervisors would observe and ask, "How did you get Bob to perform like that? He was so willing to talk to you and admit errors and make corrections. I can't get him to do anything I want." After hearing this sort of comment many times, and talking about how valuable a positive coach training would be for so many managers, Judy asked me to develop her method of coaching into the program we call The Positive Coach Approach.

In this book, we can only ask and hope for more active participation by upper managers during training programs, so they will know and understand the skills and attitudes their people are learning. By showing their interest during the training process, managers lend heavy credibility to the importance of learning and adapting to the data presented.

And, here is the good news: Any manager or coach, who's willing to learn and adopt the techniques set forth in this book can dramatically improve call center agents' performance quickly and permanently. Using this exceptional approach to active ongoing coaching, managers and coaches can accomplish astonishing, miracle-like results!

The Positive Coach Approach is truly unique in that it provides a clearly charted course of action. It's a course for anyone charged with the task of improving call center performance in the form of customer satisfaction, increased sales, shorter call times, and greater employee satisfaction. This book is a teaching guide that will lead you through what to do, why to do it, and how to do it.

This method of coaching eliminates the stress on coaches and agents that's typically associated with the perceived need for constructive criticism. In other words, it's a guaranteed, proven way to get more and better results through a kinder and gentler approach to performance improvement. The process works best by using pre-recorded calls that coaches and agents listen to together to mutually assess positive aspects as well as define challenges for improvement.

Positive coaching is an easy way to guide agents to attain rapid and lasting performance improvement in both of the important elements of call handling: compliance and skills.

1) **Compliance.** These are requirements that are imposed by legal necessities and/or company policy. *Compliance items are those that are most strictly monitored by quality control organizations "on the lookout to catch 'em doing something wrong."* Positive coaching makes correcting compliance items seem like less of a "policing action" by eliciting agreement, understanding and a willingness to make required changes to comply.

2) **Skills.** These include communication, human interaction and persuasive ability skills, and it's the area where the biggest payoffs in increased revenues and customer satisfaction can be achieved. If every agent making or taking calls in a center could be perceived by customers as a knowledgeable, qualified consultant, can you imagine what an impact that would have on revenues and company image? Positive coaching preceded by effective skills training can make that capability a reality!

The Positive Coach Approach has been designed to stand on four major foundational imperatives. To become proficient in it, managers and coaches must understand and embrace the philosophy and background of the process as outlined in each foundational block.

## Foundational Imperative #1: Four Building Blocks

Managers and coaches must adhere to the attitudinal elements (or ingredients) that make up the Four Building Blocks of positive coaching: intention, relationship, discipline and skill. By intending to be successful, developing mutually beneficial relationships, practicing self-discipline, and use appropriate communications skills, you will become a positive coach.

## Foundational Imperative #2: The LAMA Technique©

This technique will no doubt become your most useful and rewarding tool in interacting with everyone in your life, agents as well as peers, subordinates, superiors, family and friends. For our purposes, the LAMA Technique will enable you to initiate and maintain a constructive dialog with agents, thereby avoiding the tendency to "talk down to", preach or criticize instead of coaching. Your skillful use of this technique will allow you to affect great changes and improvements in the performances of agents you coach.

## Foundational Imperative #3: Eight Guiding Principles

The Eight Guiding Principles are the basic philosophy employed in establishing the "what to do, why to do, and how to do" elements of the Positive Coach Approach. These principles will facilitate your efforts to create and maintain a safe and consultative environment, build self-esteem, maintain an adult training environment, delegate responsibilities accordingly, set appropriate timelines, reach bilateral agreements, and ask the right questions.

## Foundational Imperative #4: The High Five

The High Five is a clearly defined set of five steps that provide coaches with a fail-proof agenda for conducting successful coaching sessions. This is one of the truly unique elements of this coaching book. Many instructional books will tell you what you should do, and why you should do it, but most fail to focus on telling you how to do it! If you follow the High Five, you are assured of successful, positive coaching experiences every time!

# Chapter Two
# Today's Management Issues

## Managers Are Rarely Trained to Coach.

Throughout the call center industry, managers traditionally have been trained in leadership, administrative and management skills. Does it seem like something is missing? You're right! Call center managers are seldom trained in coaching skills...and certainly not in positive coaching skills. Coaching is all about improving agent performance; it's up to managers, trainers and coaches to make sure agents have every tool to do their job well.

### The necessary tools are found in TRAINING and POSITIVE COACHING.

Because agent performance is the challenge that you will be dealing with most often, it's important to understand why coaching is the answer. Training and coaching go hand-in-hand. Once training is complete and the information on the "how to" is conveyed, it takes coaching to turn that information from ideas and concepts into performance.

## Why is Coaching the Answer?

1. Why is positive coaching the answer to the challenge of improving agent performance?

**Positive coaching** always acknowledges agents, and commends them for their willingness to do the work well. Agents will feel supported and inspired by your willingness to share quality time and experience with them.

2. What results can you achieve from using this unique coaching approach?

**Positive coaching** rapidly and dramatically improves the skill of all agents. This frees up valuable time for managers and coaches, who know they can rely on their people for excellent performance without constant supervision.

3. What can positive coaching do for the call center?

For the call center, positive coaching:

- Brings in more revenue, thereby improving financial results
- Increases goodwill and satisfaction among customers
- Makes agents' jobs more rewarding and pleasant
- Provides personal satisfaction and growth for agents and coaches

# Discovering Reasons for Substandard Performance

The biggest coaching challenge is usually agents' performance or lack thereof. Experience tells us there are really only three reasons that people don't perform well:

1. They can't do the job.
2. They won't do the job.
3. They don't know how to do the job.

Through positive coaching, you'll discover the true reasons for underachievement in handling calls. However, dealing with people who simply can't perform or who won't perform must not be attempted through coaching. These issues should be handled at a higher level of management or through human resources organizations.

> **Those who can't do the job:** This could mean the wrong people were hired for or promoted to jobs that are too difficult for them, or jobs that don't fit their personality or behavioral style. This is an HR and a management issue.
>
> **Those who won't do the job:** Usually, these people are smart enough and trained enough, but they just won't do it. Resistance of this type often stems from attitudinal differences with a supervisor, or lack of belief in the product or service being sold. Someone specially trained in counseling should handle this issue.
>
> **Those who don't know how to do the job:** It can be difficult to identify people who belong in this category vs. those who fall in one of the previous two categories. In most cases, we feel it's best to give people the benefit of the doubt, assuming they are capable but lacking in training or

practice. Since this is a new and positive process for agents, its use may save some of them from falling into one of the other two categories. It could happen!

## The Challenge for Managers

For call center managers, finding the time to coach is among the biggest challenges.

At first, your coaching sessions will take longer because you will be in uncharted waters; you'll be using a process that is unfamiliar to both you and your agents. As you practice your skills, and agents get used to their part in the process, it will require less and less time to complete coaching sessions. Using positive coaching will actually free up substantial quantities of time you currently spend handling problems that your agents could be taking care of for you. If your agents are performing well, then your time can be used more effectively in other areas.

Managers often are reluctant to initiate coaching, because they believe they'll end up merely teaching or re-enforcing training issues. Most managers feel they don't have the time or resources to do this efficiently. What they don't realize is that identifying training issues is a common and recognized side effect of coaching. Once you've identified a problem stemming from a lack or misuse of training, you can use your time more efficiently for coaching. You can stop coaching on that subject and set up a time for specific training to address a particular issue. As a result, your time can be used for coaching on previously learned skills rather than one-on-one training.

When you…

- Make the time
- Recognize the difference between training and coaching issues
- Identify whether agents "can't do," "won't do" or a "don't know how"

…positive coaching really pays off!

The bottom line is that as a manager, you owe it to the success of your call center and your individual agents to find the time to coach them in the skills they need to perform to your expectations. Training alone is simply not the answer; it's a good start, but using this innovative coaching approach to work with agents on a one-on-one basis will ensure they are actually using the tools they have been taught—in the right ways—on a regular basis.

# Chapter Three
# Three Simple Ways to Coach

When you are working with people, and you are told that there is just one correct way to do something, you should be suspect. It is always more effective to have more than one way to do something. Thus, we will not tell you that there is only one right way to coach… but there are three types of coaching that have been proven to work extremely well in most call centers.

- The first way we call <u>walk-by coaching</u>.
- The second way is <u>side-by-side coaching</u>, most of you may be doing this already.
- The third way is <u>consultative coaching</u>, on which we will primarily be focused.

The heaviest emphasis will be put on consultative coaching because it is the cornerstone of positive coaching. The methodology to conduct consultative coaching sessions is contained within the chapters that follow. You might notice that some of the lessons from consultative sessions will also apply to walk-by and side-by-side coaching.

## Walk-by Coaching

Walk-by coaching is performed just as you may have figured from its name; you walk by agents, listen to their communication, and then provide feedback. The most important feature of walk-by coaching—one that's critical—is that it must be positive. We've all heard "Praise in Public and Discipline in Private," yet many of us have done just the opposite for the sake of saving time and energy.

Being a positive coach requires you to keep to the "Positive in Public" rule. Many of you are probably doing this on occasion, but one of your goals when you commit yourself to this coaching approach should be to do even more positive walk-by coaching.

Positive feedback from walk-by coaching works well for two reasons: 1) it's immediate and 2) it's complimentary. Agents are always in need of acknowledgment; no one gets enough. In addition, getting immediate feedback for a job well done reinforces the behavior while it's still fresh in agents' thoughts. And, remember that the way you reward agents for good performance does not have to be extravagant. Consider the following story, which I came across while learning about feedback and acknowledgment:

*The Golden Banana Award. A Hewlett-Packard Company engineer burst into his manager's office in Palo Alto, CA to announce he'd just found the solution to a problem the group had been struggling with for many weeks. His manager quickly groped around his desk for some item to acknowledge the accomplishment and ended up handing the employee a banana from his lunch with the words, "Well done.*

*Congratulations!" The employee was initially puzzled, but over time the Golden Banana Award became one of the most prestigious honors bestowed on an inventive employee.*

Simple Awards Still the Best

© 1997 by Bob Nelson

How exactly do you perform a positive walk-by? Here are some ideas and guidelines:

- Use only positive feedback.
- Listen for the "good stuff."
- Take a minute to praise good behavior.
- Be specific about what you heard. (You'll learn more on how to do this in the High Five Method.)
- For a good opener, you might say, "I loved the way you opened that phone call. You made the customer feel like a friend who was invited in. You made him feel right about calling us. Thank you for that great opener."
- Give pocket prizes: movie tickets, lunch passes, candy or treats…or whatever works best for your team.
- Make walk-by coaching a habit:
    - Set timelines for yourself. Keep on the move, so you won't get caught spending too much time on this activity.
    - Don't sit down! This way, more agents can get positive attention in a short amount of time.
    - Walk different paths each day to lunch, breaks, etc., so you can hear different agents to praise.
- Give yourself 15 minutes a day for walk-by coaching:
    - 15 minutes before lunch
    - 15 minutes before a break
    - 15 minutes before closing time or shift change

By scheduling your walk-by coaching time, you can assure yourself of spending 15 minutes out on the floor creating a positive atmosphere. You may find that your team looks forward to that 15 minutes of positive coaching and will miss it when scheduling doesn't allow for it.

Walk-by coaching allows you to create a "safe environment" for your team to grow, learn and perform in. Instead of thinking, "Here comes the boss I better do it right," your team may be thinking, "Here comes my chance to get a free lunch"! You'll be facilitating a safe place for agents to show off their skills instead of hiding from you.

Let's stop here to make an important point. Many of you may have had the opportunity to hear agents say something blatantly incorrect as you've walked through your call center. While it is important to deal with that, during your walk-by coaching exercise, you're only going to deal with the positive things you hear. This is not the time to make corrections. If you hear something that is incorrect, it is a counseling issue that must be handled privately.

**Walk-by coaching must only be POSITIVE.**

## Side-by-Side Coaching

Side-by-side coaching is different from walk-by coaching in that it's more formalized; you sit down with an agent to provide coaching on specific skills. This method has both pros and cons. It's especially useful when agents are new, or there is something new to everyone, so it's safe to learn in front of others.

Side-by-side is best when used for:

- Teaching and assessing technical skills
- Demonstrating or explaining the use of the computer
- Giving directions to new hires
- Providing new product information
- Demonstrating changes in phone equipment or software applications

The common denominator of these suggested uses of side-by-side coaching is that there's no expectation of mastery, since new information is being introduced.

Side-by-side has a downside:

- It doesn't generally provide a safe environment for coaching and learning.
- It doesn't provide for privacy.
- It may result in critical difficulty, since it's often unpleasant for agents to be coached or corrected in front of others.
- There is often no tape recording available to demonstrate the issue being coached.

Unless you can coach side-by-side and maintain a safe environment, it is recommended that most coaching be done in the last way we will discuss—and our strongest recommendation—which is consultative, positive coaching.

## Consultative Coaching

Consultative coaching is where you will fully apply the lessons that you will learn in the chapters that follow.

In short, consultative coaching works because:

- It maintains a working, long-term relationship.
- It's private, consultative and supportive.
- It calls for using a developmental action plan for agents' success and improvement.
- It's recommended that it be done regularly—on a weekly basis—using pre-recorded calls.

Before we can address the process of consultative coaching, we must first explain the "approach" to our coaching method, which has four foundational elements:

Foundational Imperative #1: Four Building Blocks

Foundational Imperative #2: The LAMA Technique©

Foundational Imperative #3: Eight Guiding Principles

Foundational Imperative #4: The High Five

We will express ideas about listening and what to listen for, and then we will get into the background and the specifics of the Positive Coach Approach.

# Chapter Four
# Foundational Imperative One: Four Building Blocks

Let's get into the "meat" of positive coaching. The first foundational imperative we'll be introducing you to is our Four Building Blocks:

- Intention
- Relationship
- Discipline (meaning Self-Discipline)
- Skill

We'll examine each element in detail, and then discuss how they must work together to make your coaching efforts more productive.

Many changes have occurred in the training industry; one of the biggest is the realization of the importance of having the ability to recognize what works and what doesn't work. The days of repeating what you did before and expecting to get different results are over. It's time to make sure the right and proper things are taught and used in the call center.

Over the years, many training ideas have been implemented; some have worked and some haven't. Out of this experience have come our thoughts that you must have certain elements in every phone call. The **Intention** to produce results must be present in the mind of every coach. The **Relationship** between agents and coaches must be positive and safe for agents to learn and grow. There must be an element of **Discipline** to learn new things and apply them to the daily business. And, agents and coaches must have the **Skills** needed to be efficient and productive.

Let's look at these concepts, one-by-one.

## Intention

Intention is defined as *"a determination to accomplish a specific thing or act; to be determined in advance."* Put another, simpler way, it's what you mean to do. For example, when you leave work at the end of the day, you intend to go home, or to the gym, or wherever you go. Another example is that you intend for your children to get a good education, become solid citizens of the community, and so on.

The things you intend to have happen may not always work out the way you planned or visualized, but if your intention is strong and positive, things are more likely to turn out the way you want.

"To be determined in advance" is an important part of the definition of intention. If you are truly determined in advance, you will take action to ensure your intention becomes reality. Consider intention to have three components: a goal, a willingness to act, and a plan of action.

My mother's intention was to have all her children attend the college of their choice.

- Her goal was to earn the money to put us through school.
- Her willingness was to do what it takes to earn more.
- Her action item was, as a realtor, to sell more houses.

*I am the youngest of three and we are each a year apart, so we would be entering college three years in a row. My eldest brother, Richard, had high aspirations; he attended Notre Dame University. My second brother, Stephen, attended San Diego State University, and I attended California State University, Northridge. We all graduated from these schools.*

*My mother's intentions were very strong. She needed to make enough additional money to send us each to our desired school. Tuition was quite expensive, quite a bit more than she was making in real estate. Her intention was to earn enough for our education and for her to live on. To earn the money she needed, she had to sell more. The four years when Richard was attending Notre Dame were the four most successful years she ever had. As soon as Richard was out of school, her real estate sales and income dropped. She no longer had the intention to sell a lot of houses. She could sell an average number of houses and still put Stephen and me through school. It was not a conscious choice, but her intention was not as strong and as defined as it had to be while Notre Dame was still in the picture.*

What this example illustrates is that if you don't really take the steps required to move things along in the direction of your intention, you probably won't achieve what you want. With respect to coaching, you'll definitely find it more rewarding and productive if you intend that agents will react positively. Your own mental attitude will be seen as one to reflect and not reject or resist.

Creating outstanding results and consistent performance in the positive coaching process requires a major commitment. If you have the intention to make the coaching process succeed, you will succeed in attaining the positive results you expect.

To put this into the three-fold version of intention, you could say:

Your intention is to better your team by using positive coaching.

- Your goal is building a strong, skilled staff of agents.
- Your willingness is to do what works by learning this new approach to coaching.
- Your action item is to coach using the lessons learned in this book.

Your commitment to achieving results must consist of:

- Having the intention to produce results
- Setting targets and goals to measure the achievements of the agents you coach.
- Obtaining the proper support from:
  - Management
  - Trainees
  - Other coaches
  - Available technology

Some tips to help you build your intention are:

1) **Make it a game.** Set targets for specific accomplishments. Notice and keep score of what worked in your coaching sessions when you attained positive results and what didn't work when you attained negative results. This is vital to your success.

2) **Dwell on the rewards** of reaching your goals. How will you be affected? This can include getting promoted, increasing self-esteem, receiving recognition or acknowledgment, seeing mediocre performers begin to excel, etc.

3) **Build a strong belief** in the service you are performing and the effect it's having on your agents.

4) **View yourself as a value generator.** You really can make a dramatic difference in agents' lives!

5) Make a strong **commitment** and **intend** to succeed.

## Relationship

In the coaching process, it's very important to build and maintain warm and trusting relationships with the agents you coach. This is sometimes referred to as "rapport," which is defined as: *"a close or sympathetic relationship showing agreement and harmony."* Relationship is *"the mode of connection between one person and another."*

The key to establishing a relationship and rapport that will last lies in the ability to create what is called "a safe environment." Agents can be made to feel uncomfortable or "unsafe" during the coaching process if they perceive the coach to be glib, arrogant, sarcastic, impatient or bored. It's very important to use an honest, sincere, and unhurried attitude and tone.

Convey a feeling of willingness to serve. Make agents feel they are talking with someone who wants them to succeed and enjoy their jobs. The goal is to have the agents like and respect you, and if you achieve that goal, your job is going to be much easier.

When it comes to positive coaching, we have two sayings that summarize the intended relationship:

- Never make agents feel wrong or stupid.
- Always make agents feel right and smart to work with you.

### This is probably the most important concept in this book!

These sayings have been around for a while and they've been in my life since childhood. Why I say they are so important is because they're not only applicable to work; they can make a real difference in your life. When we do our training around the country, this is the concept we get the most comment on. People find this to be a life lesson.

When we teach this concept in training, it really is more like "Never make *anyone* feel wrong or stupid" and "Always make the *other person* right and smart." Sounds simple, but it's not. The easiest way to explain it is to give you a real-life example and then show you how it can apply to you as person and to your work as a positive coach.

Although I have known these rules since childhood, I sometimes make people feel wrong. And guess what? Sometimes, so do you. So does everyone. We cannot stop ourselves. No one takes any action without thinking they are *right* for taking it. Everyone wants to be right!

*The elderly woman driving 65 mph in the fast lane is right! She is going the speed "limit," the maximum speed allowed by law. She must be right.*

*The man driving in-and-out through traffic like he is moving pieces on a checkerboard is right. He can change lanes safely and get where he needs to be quickly. He must be right.*

*I am driving along fully aware of the amount of traffic on the road, the weather conditions, and my personal driving ability. I am driving at 80 mph. But I am safe. I must be right.*

How can we all be right? I think the elderly woman and the checkerboard man are wrong, but they don't agree! I'm not saying that anyone in this example is right or wrong. What I am saying is that if I had to work with or build relationships with these people, I would not be allowed to make them *feel* wrong or stupid.

You must learn to communicate without judgment, either in your words or tone. It's important not to use sarcasm. Instead, state clearly what it is you want agents to know.

If you want a safe environment where agents can learn and grow, you must make them feel right as you teach and coach them. This is the only way to obtain the results both of you want.

Here's a short example of practical use within a positive coaching context.

*You hear the agent, John, do something incorrectly on the phone call. John didn't ask if the customer needed further assistance at the end of the call.*

*The following statement makes John feel WRONG:*

*John, why didn't you ask "Is there anything else I can help you with?" You know you're supposed to do that on every call. It is on the Quality Assurance check sheet.*

*The following statement—while getting the same message across—doesn't make John FEEL wrong:*

*John, I noticed you didn't ask "Is there anything else I can help you with?" What happened on that call that caused you to make that decision?*

Agents don't grow if made to feel wrong or unintelligent in their choices. A great coach will work with agents to make them either feel right about their current actions or feel right about changing them. An agreement will then be made on what will be different next time. When the agreement is made, agents and coaches can both expect bigger and better things. Making agents *RIGHT* works!

## Discipline

When we say discipline, we mean self-discipline. When learning anything new, it's been noticed by us that it takes some form of change and the energy to perform. It's like exercise; most of us don't like the concept, but if we want change in our energy level it is advisable to do some exercise to make it happen. The same theory works in learning the techniques in this book and in this specific coaching course.

You'll generate much more success if you use the concept of self-discipline, which is honed through significant practice. If you want to become the finest coach and produce the highest results, you'll have to practice the methodology in this program…and that takes self-discipline.

You've probably heard the following: one man asks another on the streets of New York City, "How do you get to Carnegie Hall?" The New Yorker answered, "practice, practice, practice." The same goes for those of us who wish to learn a new skill. Whether you want to play the piano in front of thousands of people in Carnegie Hall or simply sit in a chair and observe the performance, this concept doesn't change. If you want to do something better than you are doing it now, you'll have to practice.

In addition to practicing your coaching skills, you'll also be asking your agents to practice their new skills and to demonstrate to you after they've practiced that they can perform. Your self-discipline will be especially tested as you aspire to perfect the coaching techniques covered in the chapters that follow; you'll be learning a whole new way to communicate and converse.

## Skill

This final building block element is the one that requires the most discipline. The skills required to be a positive coach can be written down in this book and read by you, but the concept of communication with *intention* to produce results—without making agents ever *feel wrong or stupid*—will require that you learn and apply this four-step method.

The next chapter introduces a core positive coaching skill, the LAMA Technique, which stands for listen, acknowledge, make a statement, and ask a question. Your ability to put this skill to work will go a long way toward determining your success as a positive coach.

You can do this! Make your job easier and communications more clear. Take the next step and communicate with the intention to never make agents feel wrong or stupid. Learn and practice the LAMA Technique and the other skills introduced in this book. Be the positive coach you want to be.

# Chapter Five

# Foundational Imperative Two: The LAMA© Technique

The Positive Coach Approach depends a great deal on the way coaches talk to agents. A special skill called the LAMA Technique is the foundation of the conversation necessary for all effective communication. It is a systematic way to initiate and maintain a productive dialogue between coaches and the people being coached (agents). The technique utilizes four steps that appear simple, but require practice to be mastered.

The power of the technique lies in the systematic way it gives agents a "feeling of being cared about" and, at the same time, enables coaches to control the conversation and the pace of the coaching session. The Positive Coach Approach uses the technique to guide agents down the path that best serves their development.

The technique does not eliminate, minimize or negate agents' ideas. Rather, it encourages agents to actively participate in the coaching process. This sounds like it would make coaching take longer, but it actually makes sessions shorter and more to the point. Coaches keep the conversation moving in a positive and caring way by initiating a dialogue—asking questions and listening to the responses. This process enables coaches to gather information, develop rapport, and observe attitudes and issues associated with agents' performance.

In the coaching process, initiating the conversation is easy. The interaction will be most effective, however, if coaches are thinking about agents' needs and how to facilitate developing skills to meet them. The coach must *intend* to produce results.

For many years, the LAMA Technique was taught to sales and customer service agents as a way to manage the sales or service conversation. Now, we are teaching the LAMA Technique as a way to manage the coaching conversation. This proven method of conversation does it all!

The LAMA Technique gives coaches the ability to control conversations with agents. For example, it gives coaches a method of getting back to the agenda if agents show a tendency to ramble or stray from the desired path of the coaching process.

When practiced and used until it becomes a habit, the LAMA Technique will be your communication skill of choice. It can be used in all conversations; it is not reserved just for coaching. It's a miracle how well it works with peers, subordinates, family and friends.

People engaged in pleasant, two-way conversations tend to establish a relationship and rapport. In all situations, but especially in coaching, it's highly beneficial to the rapport-development process if a pleasant, mutual relationship is initiated at the outset.

**Meaningful relationships cannot be built using intimidation and manipulation.** A focus on honest, open intentions and common sense tends to create communication patterns that endear agents to coaches and can cement that relationship for life. Coaches who use skills like the LAMA Technique will communicate in a manner that generates cooperation and understanding. Coaches who think they can communicate have a very good chance of doing exactly that; those who think there is no way to communicate with agents or have no desire to do so, will need to work harder.

**Nothing can ensure success more than the ability to communicate well.** People on both sides of a dialogue see themselves as stronger, their personal esteem is enhanced and their attitudes are improved when they demonstrate strong interpersonal skills.

## The ABCs of the LAMA Technique

The LAMA Technique is a simple, four-step process. It's similar to learning to ride a bicycle; it takes some practice, but once you learn it, you'll never forget how to do it. Proficient use of the technique requires developing skill in doing things we sometimes take for granted or feel we already know.

The four LAMA Technique steps are:

- Listen
- Acknowledge
- Make a Statement
- Ask a Question

Following these steps will dramatically increase coaches' abilities to communicate effectively.

## LAMA Step One: Listen

Listening requires that coaches hear and understand what's said in every element of a conversation.

Learning to listen effectively facilitates hearing nuances and gathering information that may have previously been missed. To listen effectively, coaches must shut out all judgment and evaluation, as well as any other clutter in their heads while agents are speaking.

This means:

1) Be completely with and attentive to the agents being coached; permit no distractions.
2) Actually hear and understand what agents are trying to convey.
3) Detect the hidden messages such as anger, frustration, boredom, fear, or anxiety.
4) Notice agents' pace and tone to determine personality style.

All of these listening "action items" are important, but coaches should take special notice of the last one, as noticing pace and tone allows coaches to tailor their responses to match agents' styles and abilities to grasp new performance concepts.

To be a good listener, follow these tips:

- **Prepare in advance.** Have everything you need available and organized so you can pay attention to agents.

- **Limit distractions.** Clear nonessential items from the area where the coaching will take place. Avoid phone calls and interruptions of any type as much a possible.

- **Think like an agent.** Do a little role reversal in your mind to better understand agents' points of view.

- **Limit your own talking.** Ask questions instead.

- **Listen for emotional needs**. Words may be spoken that convey anger, frustration, boredom, fear and anxiety.

- **Don't jump to conclusions.** Leave judgments behind. *Never make agents feel wrong or stupid.*

- **Don't dismiss agents' ideas.** Try to understand why thoughts have been voiced instead of tuning agents out, even if you don't agree with what they're saying.

- **Concentrate.** Focus on agents' needs.

- **Don't interrupt.** Always let agents finish what they are saying.

## LAMA Step Two: Acknowledge

The second step in the LAMA Technique is to acknowledge agents' questions, thoughts or ideas. This very important step works two ways. First, it physically and verbally tells agents their coaches are listening, and second, it psychologically acknowledges agents' needs, wants, ideas or complaints. Remember that communication is a two-way street; true communication is hearing and understanding, and then letting the other person know you heard and understood.

Acknowledgment is a vital part of any communication. It lets agents know their coaches are paying attention. It gives them a feeling of "being heard." It makes them feel they are really cared for and their coaches are ready to respond to their needs and wants in a very serious way.

In face-to-face conversation, verbal acknowledgments can be complemented with visual acknowledgments. Coaches can look into agents' eyes, nod in agreement or shake their heads in disagreement. If coaches do not show interest and understanding in what agents are saying, agents will become sensitive to the neglect immediately; they will then feel wrong or stupid because their comments haven't elicited a response. *This is an unfulfilled expectation* and makes for an unsafe environment.

Acknowledgment helps to create a safe environment. Expressing a caring attitude can make the difference between ordinary and extraordinary coaching. Using a short phrase to express understanding demonstrates that agents have been heard, which generates a feeling of safety. When coaches listen and then acknowledge what was said, agents will feel good about having decided to participate fully in the positive coaching process. Any fear agents may have had about talking to coaches begins to disappear and a safe environment is created. Instead of being *constructively criticized*, agents' points of view are heard and then incorporated into the coaching process.

If you want agents to look forward to coaching sessions, use the acknowledgment step generously. It's an easy way to make agents feel right, smart and willing to cooperate fully in the coaching process. You should practice this art of acknowledgment and make it a part of your normal conversation. Take the time to acknowledge others.

There are three ways to do the acknowledgment step using the LAMA Technique:

1) **Playback.** Repeat or parrot what agents say.

> Example: Coach says, "Bill, if I understand you correctly, you said (repeat agent's words), right?"

2) **Paraphrase.** Say the same thing, only differently. Use agent feedback to see if what you paraphrased is correct.

> Example: Agent says, "I'm not sure if I said the right thing to that customer." Coach says: "Okay, I understand. You aren't sure of what you could have said to that customer in this situation."

3) **Use short words and expressions.** While agents are talking, it's appropriate to interject short words or phrases.

> Example: Coach says, "Yes, I understand, okay, all right, good, excellent, exactly, absolutely, etc."

> This running acknowledgment tells agents their coaches are interested and understand their line of thinking. It also provides coaches with extra time — that fraction of a second that might be necessary to compose an additional question or comment to aid the coaching process.

# LAMA Step Three: Make a Statement

After coaches listen to agents and acknowledge they've heard what's been said, it's time to move to step three of the LAMA Technique. This step requires coaches to use declarative statements to deliver messages to agents, which results in a conversation. The best statements will:

- Paraphrase what agents said for clarification purposes
- Answer agents' questions
- Handle an objection
- Explain a situation
- Move the conversation forward

**Be a consultant. Be perceived as an expert.**

The statement part of the LAMA Technique is where coaches begin to act as guides, mentors or trainers. As conversations begin, agents will say something that allows coaches to kick off the coaching process. Coaches can simply acknowledge what they heard, then give agents a short statement explaining the situation, answering a question or responding in another appropriate way. Then they can move on to the next question.

## Use a statement to answer a question.

### Example:

Agent: "What should I have done there?"

Coach: "Hmmm, Bill. There are several different ways that you could have handled that. But rather than having me tell you how to do it, I'll bet you can think of some other ways to say _____. Think about it for a moment now that you heard _____. How might you do it differently next time?"

**Explanation:** The coach listened and acknowledged the agent's question, then made a statement that assured him that he's smart enough to come up with a solution. The coach made the agent feel right and smart when asking for advice.

This interaction describes the *principle* that responsibility for learning and growth in coaching situations lies with agents. (More detail on this in the next chapter.) Coaches can only open the door for agents to enhance themselves; agents must walk through it.

## Use a statement to handle an objection.

**Example:**

Agent: "I tried not to explain the details of XYZ because it always takes so much time."

Coach: "Yes you're right. It does take time to explain XYZ. Let me suggest that you look at it this way: When our customers are fully informed up front, they can often make decisions more quickly. It's not usually a good situation if customers feel they have to probe you to get the information they need to make a decision. It's better if you can stay in control of the path of the call. Sometimes, that can save you from repeating yourself. In this case, the customer did ask you a lot of questions about XYZ. Do you think explaining things up front might have actually saved you time with this customer?"

**Explanation:** The coach acknowledged how the agent feels about explaining XYZ and agreed that it is time consuming. He then handled the objection by offering expert advice in an alternative view, noting that it is possible to save time and trouble if an explanation is given up front, and more importantly, if control of the call is maintained. This statement makes the agent feel right and smart to change position on explaining things up front. Yet, the coach still leaves the decision to the agent. This maintains the safe environment.

## Use a statement to explain a situation.

### Example:

Agent: "I'm not sure why the company wants me to answer the customer by saying ABC."

Coach: "Okay, (Name), I'm glad you asked that. I know that the training program has not been too clear about that and it is a bit confusing. The main reason is because the message we want to give the customer about ABC is this *(explain)*. Did I explain that clearly?

**Explanation:** The coach listened and acknowledged that the agent was smart to ask for an explanation of policy. The coach made a statement agreeing that the training information is confusing and then clarified the explanation.

## Use a statement to move the conversation forward.

### Example:

Agent: "I think that was all I needed to know about ABC."

Coach: "Good, I think we're both clear on that. I want to be sure you don't have any more questions before we move on. Is there anything else you want to talk about?

**Explanation:** First the coach acknowledged what was heard. Then, to move the conversation along, he made a statement that says what is going to happen next, followed by a question.

# LAMA Step Four: Ask a Question

The last and most important step of the technique—asking a question—is designed to encourage agents to respond in ways that will increase their participation in coaching sessions. Using different types of questions, and knowing how to use them effectively, is a skill all coaches must master. Remember, the person asking the questions controls the path of the coaching conversation. In each of the previous examples, there was a question at the end of the scenario.

## Use questions to ask agents to take responsibility for determining a better course of action.

**Example:**

Agent: "What should I have done there?"

Coach: "Hmmm… Well, (Name), there are a few different ways you could have handled that. Now that you've done it one way, and heard how it sounded to the customer, what do you think are some ways you might do it differently next time?"

**Explanation:** This question is asking the agent to self-correct; the coach is asking for the agent to share his knowledge. You must *be careful* on how you phrase this question. A question like this may make the agent feel like you are *testing* his knowledge instead of requesting that he share what he knows. The reason this question works here is that in the preceding statement, the coach has voiced his belief in the agent's knowledge.

## Use a question to offer alternative solutions.

### Example:

Agent: "I tried not to explain the details of XYZ since it always takes so much time."

Coach: "Yes, you're right. It does take time to explain XYZ. When our customers are fully informed, they can often make decisions more quickly, and sometimes that can save you from repeating yourself. In this case, the customer did ask you a lot of questions about XYZ. Do you think it's better to skip the details or do you think explaining things up front would have saved you time with this customer?"

**Explanation:** This question is an alternate choice question. It is used to give the agent choices, which makes the agent feel that his opinion is valid. This question also leads the agent toward self-correction.

## Ask a verification question.

### Example:

Agent: "I'm not sure why the company wants me to answer the customer by saying ABC."

Coach: "Okay, (Name), that's a good point. I know the company has not been too clear about that; it's a bit confusing. The main reason is because the message we want to give the customer about ABC is this.... Did I explain that clearly?

**Explanation:** This question is used to verify that the agent understands what was just said. When both sides agree that things are clear, the conversation may move forward. This prevents making multiple explanations.

It's important to note how the question was phrased. The coach asked if he'd clearly explained his message, so the agent won't feel wrong or stupid if he didn't clearly receive it. This way, the burden is on the coach. It is a much better question than, "Do you understand?" That question puts the agent in an awkward place; if he doesn't understand, he has to either admit he is stupid, or lie and say he gets it so he doesn't *feel* stupid.

## Use a question to end a subject and move on.

### Example:

Agent: "I think that was all I needed to know about ABC."

Coach: "Good, I think we're both clear on that. I want to be sure you don't have any more questions before we move on. Is there anything else you want to talk about?

**Explanation:** Much like the previous example, this question helps to finish one subject and move on to the next. It works to move the conversation along in this example because of the statement that precedes it.

Your initial use of the LAMA Technique may seem a bit forced, but once you practice it, it will become a natural part of both your coaching conversations and those you have with other people in your life. You'll be amazed at the communication that results.

# Chapter Six
# Foundational Imperative Three: Eight Guiding Principles

It's time to move on to the eight principles around which the Positive Coaching Approach revolves. These principles have developed over time and some are still evolving.

*Judy's thoughts:*

*When I began coaching many years ago, I remember being very uncertain about how my methods would be received. Explaining them was difficult because most coaching was done in a completely parental way. In the beginning, I didn't ever have the management listen in to me; managers and supervisors were glad I had taken on the job of coaching and they left me alone. It dawned on me that I had a good idea when the agents with whom I was working began to respond with happy attitudes and good ideas of their own, and their supervisors noticed it, too.*

*My agenda was always the same:*

- *Make agents comfortable.*
- *Be clear about my expectations.*
- *Make sure they use the techniques taught in the training course.*

- *Show them how the training concepts work with customers.*
- *Let them know I believe in their ability to perform.*
- *Allow them to show me they can and will do what is expected in a timely manner.*
- *Set up some agreements with me as to how and when they will do the things on the performance list.*

*Agents' supervisors were parental; they had a different agenda.*

- *Point out errors.*
- *Give instructions on how to fix them.*
- *Be generally disheartened at agents' performance.*
- *Use parental commands.*
- *Provide constructive criticism.*
- *Tell agents what to say and how to say it.*
- *Mark their monitoring forms with less than best marks.*

From these thoughts, these principles were created. The coaching experience should not be parental and negative; it should be consultative and positive. Learn these principles, and live them, as you work with agents during coaching sessions.

## Principle #1: Create and Maintain a Safe Environment

There is very little opportunity for agents to develop unless coaching sessions are considered a safe environment. As the coach, you are responsible for creating that safe environment, which means agents must *feel safe* and at ease in your presence and be able to interact freely without hindrance or complication. Most coaching sessions we've observed over the years have not had safe environments.

When you can make it safe for agents to express their feelings, ideas, and solutions to problems or issues, you will see a huge difference in their commitment to grow and perform. If you make it "unsafe" or are critical of their ideas, agents are usually reluctant to offer any suggestions and will not be inclined to attempt self-correction. They will wait for you as the coach or manager to tell them what to do.

Everyone likes to think they have ideas, systems and methods that work. If you wish to obtain the highest and best results from your agents, you must create a safe environment and let the magic happen!

The most important element of a safe environment is *trust.* This means you must create an environment in which agents believe you have their best interests at heart. You must be able to convince them that you can be trusted to inform, teach, and train them in what will work best for them and for the company. Trust is the key; you must make sure agents believe you can be trusted.

When you begin your first sessions using this novel coaching approach, you may notice that agents are wary of you and may not understand that something different is about to happen. This is the right time to explain how this new method of positive coaching will affect your approach, and how it will make it easier and more pleasant for them to perform and grow.

Approach the positive coaching session with the intent to give up your personal judgments regarding the agents you are coaching. It's not easy to do that when you're supposed to be coaching someone to success, but it is precisely these judgments that get in the way of creating a safe environment. You must trust that agents want to succeed and will do what is required if appropriately guided toward that end.

The desired condition to be achieved is when agents feel free to discuss methods, ideas and suggestions in a way that can make a contribution to the company and to the situation. When this happens, you will know you are trusted. Then, all you have to do is to maintain this trust throughout your coaching sessions and enjoy watching amazing improvements in agent performance.

One way to facilitate a safe environment is to listen together with agents to tapes of the calls to be assessed. You shouldn't listen to the tapes in advance of coaching sessions; if you do, you won't be able to maintain a completely unbiased opinion. Preconceived notions don't allow for a safe environment. Make sure you don't form opinions in advance. When you tell the agents that you have not heard the call in advance, the agents are clear that you have no preconceived ideas. Then, when you ask for their input, it makes the agents feel safe and believe their input is valid. The aspect of listening to the call together promotes a mutual desire to work toward improvement.

Working together is one of the cornerstones of positive coaching. Please resist with all your might your strong tendency to want to tell agents what to do. Advice given before agents have had a chance to self-correct will be considered reprimands or criticisms of their performance. On the other hand, when you use the eight principles, which encourage self-discovery and self-correction, agents will feel important, adult and confident.

Follow these tips to help you in learning how to develop a safe environment:

- **Describe how positive coaching works.** Make sure they know that this coaching approach promotes an atmosphere of mutual trust, honesty and respect. Tell them they're going to have the opportunity to decide and participate in what they can do to improve their own performance, and that you, as a positive coach, will guide and work with them as necessary to make that happen.

- **Look for the "good stuff" and tell them about it!** Strive to notice the good and correct actions of your agents. Acknowledge them during walk-bys and in coaching sessions and any other times you hear something good. When you hear or see good behavior, tell them about it immediately, if possible, and be specific about what you heard and why you liked it. Let them know what you perceived as good and correct behavior.

- **Eliminate constructive criticism.** Nobody likes or responds well to constructive criticism, so don't use this parental approach when coaching. It does not lend itself to a safe environment; agents will fear you and dislike you for using it. When you come around to talk to them about their work, they will anticipate your attitude as being one of a parent. Instead, use adult training modes and principles. Treat your agents like the adults they are and you will obtain much better results.

- **Use positive reinforcement only.** If you hear or observe someone saying something incorrect or inappropriate, use positive reinforcement publicly and give additional feedback privately. Ask agents how they feel about what transpired. Then ask them what happened and how they might handle the situation in a better way the next time it occurs.

- **There are no right or wrong questions.** Encourage agents to ask questions. Allow them to ask any question they wish. Show interest in their ideas by asking: "What do you think?" or "How did you feel about that?" To create a safe environment, it's important to let them know that you are there for their improvement. Let them know that if they do well and look good, you do, too.

- **Encourage agents to self-discover and self-correct.** A safe environment is one in which agents can train themselves. There will be no need for negative feedback or constructive criticism. Start a process that encourages self-correction through a dialogue initiated by a series of questions.

- **Avoid asking questions you know the answer to in a way that makes agents feel wrong or stupid.** Here are examples of questions not to ask: "Don't you think you should have asked that customer for more information?" and "What do you think you did wrong on that call?" Instead, ask something that makes agents feel right and smart like these examples: "What questions could you have asked to gather more information from that customer?" and "On that call, what do you think you might have said to make it go a little more smoothly?"

- **Develop a "work together" atmosphere.** Work together for the development of agents' success. Later we will discuss exactly how to develop a progress plan in detail. Keep in mind that this not a "do what I say" situation. It's more like a partnership, where working things out together will ensure mutual success. Visualize a situation where agents work with you, not for you. After all, your focus in coaching is their career, their job, and their pending success, and you are both after the same goals. So, do it together.

# Principle #2: Create a Consultative Environment

You must strive to create a consultative-type environment, in which you and your agents engage in a dialogue, both observing, listening, and asking and answering questions. This means discussing the impressions formed by each of you to get a clear picture of strengths and weaknesses affecting agent performance. Following this procedure, you can collectively come up with recommendations and plans for perfecting techniques. A partnership needs to be formed to assist agents to learn and improve. Being consultative allows you to collaborate with agents instead of simply telling them what to do.

As the consultative partnership between you and your agents starts to form and a safe environment is created, agents will begin to take responsibility for their own growth. It's important that they gain a sense that you respect their intellect and feelings. This indicates to them that you want them to succeed, and at the same time encourages them to take on the challenges of higher and better performance on their own. You open doors with questions and agents respond with ideas and suggestions to increase their productivity and skill levels.

This is a new way of thinking for most supervisors and managers who are used to using the "finding-what's-wrong-and-telling-how-to-fix-it" technique. The consultative method will take a little longer at first, but soon agents will be combining their knowledge and experience with yours, and both of you will grow.

After a few meetings that start with a safe environment and employ a consultative environment, coaching sessions will go faster. Agents will begin in earnest to accept responsibility for their own growth and the partnership consultation strategies will develop rapidly. This new approach will most likely require some changes in your operating style, but will pay off dramatically in time saved over the year because there will be no need for repeated correction and discipline. Agents will learn quickly that you are their consultant, working with them to enhance their success, and as a consequence, the time that coaching and mentoring takes will be dramatically shortened.

To be consultative in nature, remember these rules:

- A consultative approach takes time and practice to perfect.
- Coaching sessions are an exchange of ideas.
- Be supportive by asking questions.
- Consult with agents about methods of self-correction.
- Engage agents in the concept of thinking for themselves… so you can stop doing it for them.

Your hard work will be rewarded by the formation of partnerships for success between you and your agents.

## Principle #3: Build Self-Esteem by Focusing on the Positives

Building agent self-esteem requires overt actions on your part. You must intentionally focus on the positive aspects of agent performance. If your energy level is low, and your attitude seems to be parental or critical, you won't be doing yourself any favors. Being perceived as a critical parent will not endear you to agents, and it will do nothing to build their self-esteem. What will build their self-esteem is your positive attitude and the ability to tell them what they do most of the time is right and correct!

From the moment agents perceive the positive coaching process is designed to make their performance better and their success assured, you'll notice a dramatic change in their willingness to participate with new energy. Conversely, experience shows that if agents perceive coaching as constructive criticism, they will usually put up barriers to their own successful learning. You can break down the barriers by acknowledging positive performance. If you are parental or use constructive criticism, agents may resist every word you say simply because they feel criticized.

Why maintain a positive environment? It's simple, works best, takes less time, and is less frustrating…and you keep customers satisfied and agents working at a high level in a happy environment. The results go up and the problems go down. Performance will improve and the workplace will be pleasant.

Remember that your goal is to help agents be more successful and ensure customers are more satisfied with the treatment they receive. When agents have coaches who are creating safe learning environments by being completely positive, the goals become obvious. This type of attitude is contagious and the results will prove it.

Keep these simple points in mind:

- Stay positive in the face of adversity.
- Negative energy will not work; agents often see this as an attack.
- Agents will go to their own way if they are not given positive feedback.
- Show confidence with your attitude.
- Don't be right; let agents be right, so they grow.
- Demonstrate that you are positive with sincere words and phrases.
- Constantly build self-esteem. It will pay off big time.

What will it take to end your doubt that you can actually give up being negative and learn how to be positive? What will you need to do or know for you to see that negative energy causes resistance and positive energy causes positive responses? Seeing is believing…so change your behavior and watch what happens. Let go of the negative and put in the positive; never go over to the dark side again.

If you want to know what to say and how to say it in a positive way, you will find examples in the several of the following chapters. You'll find many examples of specific words and phrases to help you coach with positive energy.

# Principle #4: Maintain an Adult Training Environment

You must have high expectations of agents to act and perform as adults. Open your mind to the fact that they want to succeed. If you maintain an adult environment and a positive attitude toward them, agents will respond as adults.

All positive coaching sessions must be based on the premise that agents want to improve their skills, perform well and do a good job.

Adult training philosophy precepts are simple!

- Be sure agents are trained in exactly what to say and how to say it.
- Make sure agents know what you expect of them; provide clear performance criteria.
- Allow agents to ask as many questions as they wish.
- Consult with agents and allow them to explain their points of view.
- Communicate clearly that you expect agents to self-correct.
- Let agents know you aren't going to be acting the part of their parent and they're expected to respond with adult behavior.

When you coach agents, treat them as equals and show that you respect their points of view whether you agree with them or not. Positive coaching is a consultative process created to help agents develop their ideas and their solutions to problems.

*Three*

adult environment is important to make sure agents
understanding and not made to feel small. Your job
give agents the guidance they need to succeed and that means
taking no joy in their weaknesses. If you can make the agents feel
right and smart to participate openly in the coaching process, your
coaching task will be much easier and more productive.

Let the adults you work with come up with their own solutions,
allow them to know you have the confidence in them and that
they have what it takes to succeed. Be sure you tell them you are
counting on them to find their own way to success.

*Recently, after having conducted a training program, I was about to
start the side-by-side follow-up coaching session. The agent and I had
just listened to a recorded call and he said, "Okay....just tell me what
I do wrong." This comment told me that he was used to his manager
making him feel wrong and probably stupid. He was used to parental
attitudes and correction by so-called constructive criticism. So, I said,
"Whoa! This will be different, I promise. I expect you to listen to yourself,
examine the call and make recommendations on the things that you
would like to correct, fix or change. I'll also expect you to find three
things you felt that you did well when you handled the customer. We're
going to spend time making sure you know how much you do right on
every phone call. Okay?" He changed instantly from a fearful person to
one who was a little skeptical but willing to give this positive coaching
method a try.*

As you use the elements of positive coaching, give your agents a
chance to discover what didn't work and acknowledge what did.
Let them demonstrate to you that they'll continue to do what works
and let go of what doesn't on their own, without you or anyone else

holding their hand. They are not like children who need assistance crossing the street; they are adults who know to look both ways and make a decision. This is the adult principle that will give you the satisfaction of knowing you are helping someone else grow into their own success and, believe me, agents will thank you for it.

Agents left home a long time ago and they didn't do it to be put into another parental situation. They did it to be on their own because they think they can be successful. You are the one to make that happen by ensuring they know what's expected and giving them the tools to succeed. Then, let them know you know they CAN and WILL do what works. This is a happy learning environment.

## Principle #5: The Responsibility to Learn and Grow Lies with Agents

Your responsibility is to sharpen agents' skills. Their responsibility is to learn, grow and use their sharpened skills to the best advantage in their jobs. Your job as a coach will be much easier if you make this distinction very clear to agents at the outset of the process.

What exactly does the word responsible mean? Unfortunately, many parents instill in their children the idea that being responsible for something is akin to taking blame for it. Responsibility simply put means: *the cause of a matter.* You should instill in agents the value of being responsible, keeping blame completely out of the picture. Blame is not an issue in the coaching environment.

Do whatever you can to help agents learn to be responsible for their own growth, learning and self-correction. If they need assistance, you're responsible for teaching them.

*In a class we had at a huge call center, we were teaching the managers about how to handle difficult agents and what to do with them using positive coaching. I asked a manager to role-play with me and she handled the given situation beautifully right up to the end where she unknowingly negated this principle.*

*At the very end of the role-play, she said: "Now, Sally, if you need any support from me, if you need any help in doing this, you just come to me with your problems and I will help you solve them. My door is always open to you and since you are the most important part of my job, I will be available to you any time, any time at all."*

*I asked her if I could come by <u>every day</u> or have her listen to my calls <u>every day</u> until I got it right. Would she do it? She said, "Oh yes, I'm happy to help you any way I can."*

*I went back into training mode and asked her to look at who is now responsible for this agent's correction? She thought for a moment and her face lit up! She said, "I broke one of the main principles, didn't I? I took on this agent's whole job and did not leave it up to her to learn on her own." She realized she was being parental; she should be leaving the responsibility up to agents.*

*She said she'd used a heart-felt system all her career and she never got the results she wanted from it. She was very kind, but she always ended up with every monkey on her back...and she'd never understood that she was doing it to herself.*

*I then went back to the principle of responsibility resting with agents (or in this case, the manager.) I asked her to redo what she said, this time making it the responsibility of the agent to grow, learn and practice. Here is what she said:*

*"Sally, you did so well on that with your ideas on how to fix this issue with the customer. You came up with a fine solution and I am proud of you. The next time you engage the customer and change the way you handled it, let me know and I'll listen to your call. I would like to acknowledge you for making the change on your own. Okay?"*

This is a lesson all big-hearted managers and supervisors need to learn. It's like teaching your child to drive; eventually you have to give them keys to the car and the job rests with them to do it right and be safe.

You can see how the principles continue to work in every situation, *including this one*. This manager just learned by hearing herself, she self-corrected and she came up with her own solution. Since she did this for herself, she learned instantly that this is the best way for her to teach and coach her agents. She realized the result will be to free up time for her administrative work and she will have time to coach more often. Wow!

The agent and the agent alone is the one who is to act on the correction needed, the method of learning and the method of growing. Learn to separate who is responsible for learning and growing from who is responsible for teaching and coaching. This will give both of you a secure place from which to operate.

## Principle #6: Timelines are Essential

During coaching sessions, you and your agents will learn to set specific, realistic and timely goals.

It's essential that agents set timely goals as to how long it will take them to change a habit, learn something completely new, or just do something they had never done before. Timelines are a requirement for growth. Agents will learn quicker when specific timeframes are set to accomplish their goals; there's nothing to shoot for when timeframes are left open ended.

Goal setting is typically challenging for agents, and new coaches may find it hard to put this component of positive coaching into practice...but this is the part that causes change. Some coaches will find it very hard to ask for this commitment because it is causing something to happen. Agents must come up with a time estimate and be responsible for changing their behavior by that self-imposed deadline. Agents need confidence in themselves and they need to know that you realize they are adults and believe they are capable of learning new things quickly. With that in mind, have your agents pick timelines that are realistic and commensurate with their skills and abilities.

You must allow agents to set their own timelines.

At times it may be difficult to set timelines that are mutually agreeable. It's typical in the coaching environment for agents to realize that coaches are usually willing to let them use their own discretion when learning new things as long as there's agreement on the timeline. At the same time, it's been our experience that agents often want a long time to learn something. It never seems to be a good idea to give them a very long time to learn a new technique or change a habit on a three-minute phone call.

Habits are hard to change. When people decide to quit smoking or go on a diet, it's always difficult because there must be a timeline involved or everyone just gives up. Since positive coaching is something meaningful—serious business—it will take a certain commitment to time. You'll learn later how to use the High Five coaching method, which requires only three new lessons a week at the most. Since there are only three things to work on at a time, setting timelines isn't as hard as you may think.

When timelines are set, you'll learn how long it takes to enact behavioral changes. What you'll see is that it seldom takes too long. It only takes a short time for agents to make up their minds to learn and a short time to practice before something that works better becomes a part of their lives. Start today and watch your agents grow quicker when dates are set for them to reach their learning goals.

## Principle #7: Use Bilateral Action Agreements

Bilateral action agreements—when you and your agents agree on the action to be taken—are an important part of positive coaching. If you want agents to act like adults, using their own wit and wisdom to learn something new, your coaching agreements will answer several questions. In addition to asking agents to make a behavioral change, you must consult and mutually agree on how they will learn and remember to make the given change, and how that will occur in a timely manner.

I like to use the principle of agreements when working with others. I heard once that "life works to the degree that you keep agreements." For instance, if you don't drive at the speed limit, you could get a ticket, or if you eat too much you'll gain weight. Those are life-principled agreements, but if you want to encourage agents to learn new things, you also need agreements.

If they haven't figured it out already, your agents will know by this activity that this coaching method is different; you'll be letting them know you plan to support their growth by making these agreements. In addition, you'll amplify that your meetings have meaning…they are meetings of adults who create a mutually safe environment, use established principles of learning, and consult with each other on the ways and means to successful results.

## Principle #8: Questions are the Key

Questions are the key that will open up any conversation. If you ask them in a way that makes agents feel good, smart and right to answer them, you'll have very good coaching sessions.

*I initially thought my methods were accepted because I was just more fun and I was an outsider providing a different experience. It was later when I realized that I did things very differently from agents' supervisors, monitors and coaches. Supervisors used subjective ways and means instead of objectives to bring about changes in behavior and it never seemed to work. Because supervisors had good intentions, they couldn't figure out what was wrong. They either did not ask questions or they asked questions that made agents feel small and foolish, and less than smart and right to answer them. Putting questions that made agents feel right and smart down on paper was the start of something big.*

You will need to be prepared to ask your agents questions throughout coaching sessions. You'll find examples of good questions throughout this book. Your questions will guide your coaching conversation.

- After giving a list of your expectations, you'll ask agents if they think you've been clear about them.

- After you hear tapes or listen to calls together, you'll acknowledge agents and ask them to self-acknowledge with more questions.

- When you're preparing to open the conversation about challenges, you'll need a few more questions.

- After that, you'll begin the self-correction stage and need a question or two to engage agents in the process of self-correction and learning.

- At the point of the session when you allow agents to come up with their own ideas on fixing situations for the future, you'll need a couple more questions, spoken in just the right way so as not to make agents feel uncomfortable. You want to do exactly the opposite, ensuring your questions demonstrate your faith in them to learn, correct, grow and improve their performance.

Knowing how to ask questions is an important component of positive coaching. You need to know what to say and how to say it to be a good coach, just as agents need to know what to say and how to say it to be excellent customer service representatives or salespeople. We have provided a selection of appropriate questions in the Appendix.

## Simple Solutions Work Best

There's a lot to learn in this book, but much of it boils down to using these eight principles. They work!

- Create and Maintain a Safe Environment
- Create a Consultative Environment
- Build Self-Esteem by Focusing on the Positives
- Maintain an Adult Training Environment
- The Responsibility to Learn and Grow Lies with Agents
- Timelines are Essential
- Use Bilateral Action Agreements
- Questions are the Key

Give up ideas and thoughts that don't work and you'll start to have coaching sessions that:

- Enlighten
- Move
- Cause growth
- Allow agents to perform to their own best ways

You'll be so happy you learned these ways and means to coaching… and your agents will be delighted, too. By becoming a positive coach, you'll realize the best reward of all: the long-term success of your agents.

# Chapter Seven
# Learn To Listen

## Listen for Subtleties

Good consultative coaching requires learning to listen actively for subtle nuances in the conversation between agents and customers. As a positive coach, you must learn to listen to both parties. Most coaches listen only to agent performance, but it is equally important to listen to customers and how they react to what agents say. A lot can be learned from customer responses.

When listening to recorded calls, coaches must learn to listen for all the good things that agents do well. The positive coach will be prepared to acknowledge agents for "the good stuff," rather than merely focusing on areas to improve. The positive coach must also learn to recognize the subtle indicators that a barrier exists, or comes up, in conversations between customers and agents.

### We refer to these indicators as "STOPS."

Stops are places in conversations where something occurs—fostered by either agents or customers—that stops or impedes the flow of conversation. A conversation is like a tide that ebbs and flows; when a stop occurs, the conversation loses that fluid motion.

As you review calls, active listening will enable you to praise agents for the things they do well as well as notice the stops. As a result of your use of positive coaching, agents will soon begin to recognize the stops themselves and analyze what was said or done to create them. Agents will also learn to recognize the positive behaviors that keep the conversation fluid: the good stuff. These are major steps in agents learning to *self-correct* and *build self-confidence.*

## Listening to Customers

The positive coach needs to be able to listen not only to agents, but to customers as well. When listening to calls, you can immediately detect how well agents are performing by listening carefully to what customers are saying and how they say it. That's why we suggest you listen to the customer first. Answer this question when you listen to customers to help you find both the good stuff and the stops:

### What caused the customer to act differently?

Here are some examples of things that *customers* may do that will indicate that agents have done something **well** on calls:

- Customers sound delighted, satisfied or pleased. This may be indicated by their willingness to tell a story, give out information, or otherwise be responsive and conversant.
- Customers display good moods. They may sound grateful.
- Customers show confidence in agents and thank them by name.

These fall into the good stuff category, and are things you'll use to acknowledge agents.

Here are some examples of the stops that you will hear by listening to customers:

- Customers do not speak, resulting in dead air.
- Customers change their tone from pleasant to irritated.
- Customers are abrupt or rude.
- Customers suddenly ask for the price.
- Customers interrupt agents for any reason.
- Customers abruptly hang up.
- Customers don't know what to say or do; they hesitate or are uncertain.
- Customers don't know the answer to an agent-posed question.
- Customers refuse to give an answer to an agent-posed question.
- Customers act defiant or righteous.

Overcoming some of these stops is fairly obvious. For example, when customers don't know the answer to an agent-posed question, or refuse to provide an answer, you need to review the question, as it's probably not phrased in a way to facilitate customer response. Using the skills learned through positive coaching will help overcome the other, less straightforward stops.

## Listening to Agent Performance

In your coaching experience, you probably already focus on agent performance. You can ask the question:

**What is it that agents have done to create
good experiences for customers?**

Let's start by looking at a list of things that can apply in most call centers to good agent performance. These are things you may want to keep in mind when acknowledging agents:

- Excellent call path control
- Asked appropriate questions
- Very little dead air
- Made suggestions
- Refocused the customer
- Seeded the sale
- Determined customer needs
- Maintained pleasant adult tone

Next, when listening to agent performance, also ask this question:

**What have agents done or not
done to cause the stops?**

- Was it something the agent said?
- Was it the tone of voice that changed the environment from safe to unsafe?
- Was it the phrasing of a question that made the customer uncomfortable?
- Was the question impertinent?
- Was the question rhetorical?

- Was the question too direct…or too indirect?
- Was the question a setup to make the customer do something?
- Did the question lead the customer in a way that made him feel manipulated?
- Was the customer rushed?

Sometimes the stop is created more by the question than by specific performance. For example, what we think is a good question can cause stops for customers. This may depend on the question itself or just the situation or frame of mind that customer is in at the time.

> For example: "What is your birth date?"
>
> Depending on the situation, asking this may actually irritate customers.
>
> Some people really don't like to reveal their age.

This is a simplistic way of explaining that a question may be perceived as intrusive. So, questions must be asked gently and set up (or explained why they are being asked) to avoid potential stops from occurring.

You can hear new things everyday and that is why we simply call them stops, meaning that the flow of the conversation was stopped. Sometimes agents unknowingly cause stops or customers stop because of something agents have no control over.

What can the positive coach do about stops? When you put the lessons in this book into practice, you will know how to coach agents about correcting stops. The starting place is to take responsibility for them. This means taking ownership of the problem or the reason the conversation changed in a negative way or even came to a dead halt.

This does not mean assessing blame; it simply means acknowledging an error has occurred. Since we cannot correct customers, we must correct our scripts, our agents' performance, and ourselves.

The important thing to know is...What caused the stop?

Only after identifying that behavior can it be corrected, using one of the tools provided in this book.

# Chapter Eight
# Foundational Imperative Four: High Five Method

## Introduction to the High Five Method

By now, you've been exposed to lots of data and background information on positive coaching, so you probably have an idea of how you'd like to approach your coaching sessions.

- Your intention will be to create a safe environment and strive to make agents feel right and smart.
- You'll call on positive coaching's eight principles and building blocks as required.
- You'll use your newly learned conversational skill, the LAMA Technique, to initiate and sustain communication and you'll be clear on what types of things to listen for.

The next logical step is to combine all these facets of positive coaching to make your coaching sessions much more successful and productive. How do you do that? Of course we have an answer for you! Just follow a simple system that we call the High Five Method, which consists of the following five steps:

- Expectations
- Acknowledgments

- Challenges
- Self-Correction
- Personal Performance Plan

These five steps, combined with the use of the four building blocks, the LAMA Technique and the eight principles, will guide your interactions with agents during coaching sessions. Each step is an important link to the next; we'll go over each in depth, and with practice and a little effort, you'll become a positive coach.

What is the High Five?

The High Five is really a meeting agenda. All meetings should have an agenda at the outset, to ensure they run smoothly and everyone involved is comfortable and safe in their roles. The High Five provides a structure for your coaching sessions.

If you've been using a form to document what occurs during coaching sessions, you may want to revise it to reflect the premise of positive coaching. It's important to give agents a copy of the form so they may take notes. This will help create a safe environment and encourage agent participation. (The McKee Motivation form is included as a reference in Appendix D)

## Step One: Expectations

Setting expectations at the outset of coaching sessions is critical. This important first step of the High Five is to establish the three criteria to be assessed on the calls you'll be reviewing. These will be the "expectations." Start to create a safe environment by making it clear that this will be the first time you've heard these calls.

Explain that although there are many criteria on a Quality Call Checklist, you will only listen for the things you've selected in any one session. This contributes to establishing a safe environment. It also sends the message that agents are good at their jobs and it's not possible to assess or to perform *every* thing *every* time.

## Choosing Expectations

Choosing expectations can be done in several ways:

- You choose all three expectations.
- Your agents choose all three expectations.
- You choose expectations together.

Since this is your first opportunity to be consultative and build agents' confidence, we suggest the third option, with the exception noted below. Asking agents for input right away can start you off on the right foot.

**Caution:** Don't let agents choose all the expectations *at first*. If they do not yet feel the safe environment, they may tend to pick the easiest items from the list of criteria. There must be some challenges presented, setting the bar high, just not so high as to be unreachable.

Here is the tricky part about expectations, and this may seem a bit confusing. After you set the expectations and listen to a specific call, you may or may not address the chosen expectations. In most cases, the expectations you're listening for will happen, but on occasion, the chosen call doesn't involve them. If this happens, it's all right. Since you'll be using the High Five and LAMA Technique, you'll be able to lead the coaching session in the direction most needed for the specific call.

The true purpose of choosing expectations is to give a focus to both you and your agents. This is the first opportunity you have to get agents involved in evaluating their own performance. By starting coaching sessions this way, you're making it safe for the agents; you're assisting them put aside the notion that their input is rarely recognized. You're also setting the stage for one of the eight principles: the Responsibility to Learn and Grow Lies with Agents.

## Choosing the Call

Some of the more sophisticated systems record all agent calls, while others record only a percentage of them; some have very limited recording ability or little control over retrieving specific calls. Here are some good ideas about choosing the calls. Which one you use depends on the recording capabilities of your particular call center.

Systems that record for training use:

- Agents choose from a list of their own calls.
- You choose from the list of calls.

If you choose, you may want to use call length as a guideline. Shorter than average calls may not have enough on them to get a feel for agent performance. Longer than average calls my have so much happening that agents may feel the need to make a laundry list of errors.

No system in place to record calls for training:

- Use a handheld tape recorder or a digital voice recorder to record actual calls in progress.

If this is the case, you should set the expectations before recording. There is a certain amount of challenge built in to this way of operating, since you'll only be recording agents' sides of calls.

It's best if you can listen to both sides of the conversation, but if you don't have the equipment, you may still coach effectively with the agent side only.

The final step in the expectations step is listening to the calls. We recommend listening to three calls or 15 minutes' worth of calls, whichever is appropriate. This is recommended so you and your agents will be comfortable that you're listening to a good sampling of their performance.

## Step Two: Acknowledgments

This will not be an entirely new concept to you, since we already discussed acknowledgments in general when you learned the LAMA Technique. You learned how to acknowledge what another person has said, and that almost no one gets enough acknowledgment. In the High Five, when we talk about acknowledgments, we are talking about complimenting a specific behavior that was done correctly or skillfully.

While you and your agents are listening to calls, write down specific things the agents do well. Note at least three things you liked. When you acknowledge agents, you'll need to give specifics about what you heard. The difference between a specific acknowledgment and a non-specific acknowledgment is like night and day.

Here's an example of a non-specific acknowledgment:

> "Your opener was very nice."

Now here's an example of a specific acknowledgement:

> "(Name), the first thing that I noticed about that call was that you gave an energetic opener. Your tone was high and when you introduced yourself you really sounded eager to help. That always sets customers at ease."

Specifics are very important when acknowledging agents. By being specific, you add credibility to the compliment. Agents can feel safe that you aren't just saying something nice to "soften the blow" of what they expect to come next.

Acknowledgments in the High Five are done in two stages.

In the first stage, you acknowledge agents. You'll tell agents two of the three things that you think they performed skillfully, saving the third for the end of the session. This way, the session always ends on a positive note.

In the second stage of acknowledging, you ask agents to self-acknowledge. Use the LAMA Technique, ending with a question that asks agents to acknowledge themselves.

For example:

> "I also heard you make the cross-sell attempt. You offered the correct companion item to the item the customer was inquiring about. Thank you. <u>So, what did you like best about that call?</u>"

You make conversations consultative in this way, by asking agents to participate. This builds their confidence and focuses the conversation on their positive performance.

The LAMA Technique will continually come into play while acknowledging. You ask agents to self- acknowledge, and they give one positive about their performance. Agents may or may not be comfortable at this point. The positive coach will use the LAMA Technique and finish with questions that ask agents to come up with more acknowledgments.

You will continue using the LAMA Technique until agents run out of things to self-acknowledge. ***This is critical!*** You should get agents to self-acknowledge at least three times, and more if you can get them to keep saying good stuff. Each time agents find something good in their performances and you get to acknowledge them for it, you apply several of the guiding principles of positive coaching.

- You are positive and build agent confidence.
- Agents are responsible for their own performance and it is positive performance!
- You demonstrate that you're treating agents as adults.
- You encourage agents to learn and grow by continuing with these positive behaviors.

## Are Agents in a Safe Environment?

If agents are safe and comfortable, they may immediately participate and tell you what they did well. This does not happen very often when you first use positive coaching; it's normal for agents to be wary. When they are unsure of their "safety," agents will say one nice thing and then try to go to the negative.

These agents are smart; they know the purpose of "coaching" in the past was all about telling them what they did wrong. So, to beat you to the punch, they figure that they will admit their transgressions up front. *Be careful* here and do not let agents get negative.

Agents are so used to having managers or supervisors coach in a "good news/bad news" scenario, that they often will say something like, "Okay, tell me what I did wrong" or "I knew I blew that part; what else should I fix?" They want to pull that Band-Aid® off fast to lessen the pain. This is where your LAMA skills will really come in handy.

You must use the LAMA Technique to acknowledge negative comments without making them a point of discussion. Then, change the subject back to a specific acknowledgment of a good behavior from the phone call. It's vital at this stage in the High Five that you do not get drawn into discussing things that challenge agents. You will discuss them later, but first you have to dwell on the positives.

Most people are hungry for acknowledgment, but they are taught not to "blow their own horn," so for some agents, this part of the coaching may be hard. You can put them at ease by using a transitional phrase followed by a question. You can say something like:

> I know it's hard to self-acknowledge and it's unusual. **(Listen, Acknowledge)**
>
> This is the way coaching will be from now on and I really want you to be able to recognize what you do well and to acknowledge yourself for it. **(Make a Statement)**
>
> So tell me, what did you like most about that call? **(Ask a Question)**

It's necessary to focus yourself and your agents on the things they do well every day; it's human nature to overlook the positives in behaviors that have been learned and applied. Almost everyone forgets that they had to learn to answer the phone, give the company name and their own name, too! This is a learned behavior that seems so ordinary that agents do not expect or even accept praise for it. These are some of the things that will be acknowledged by the positive coach.

> *When I was in school and I received a 90% on a test, I always looked at the 10% that I missed. I beat myself up for missing that 10%. What I rarely did was look over the answers that awarded me the 90%. I concentrated on the negative. Most people do. They may give a cursory*

*acknowledgment of the 90%—the good news—but they spend the majority of their energy on the 10%— the bad news.*

**With positive coaching, you'll be spending a lot more time on the good news!**

You do all this by saying something as simple as:

YES! I agree. **(Listen)**

You identified that she was ready to buy, you made your offer and then you made the attempt at the up-sell as well. **(Acknowledge)**

Thank you. That is exactly how it should be done! **(Make a Statement)**

What else did you do well? **(Ask a Question)**

When you spend the majority of coaching sessions on positives, agents will be encouraged that they are doing it right. They'll also leave sessions with improvement plans and the self- confidence that will enable them to make the necessary changes to do an even better job. The seeds of improvement are planted when you take the time to dwell on the positives and ask agents to do the same. This is why positive coaching works so well.

Here are some different ways to ask agents to self-acknowledge:

- What did you like most about the call?
- What did you think you did well?
- What was your favorite part about the call?
- What else?

## Step Three: Challenges

Now that you have spent time on the acknowledgments, or the good stuff, it's time to turn your attention to challenges. There will almost always be things that agents could have done better. When discussing challenges, you need to use words that indicate agents' abilities and skills are good and can be improved rather than using verbiage that indicates a need to correct or fix.

While listening to calls, notice the three main things you heard that you may want agents to improve on. Write these down. Noticing areas for improvement is what you are used to doing when listening to calls. Because you are now going to ask agents to self-discover and self- correct, you may not need to use any of the challenges you note. With your interaction and use of the LAMA Technique, agents will probably discover appropriate challenges on their own. Most of us are our own worst critics.

When agents run out of things to self-acknowledge, you will utilize your LAMA skill to focus on the challenges you noticed. At this juncture, you ask questions that encourage agents to identify those challenges for themselves.

Here is an example of how to transition from acknowledgements to challenges:

> Thank you for those acknowledgments. You did do all those things well. **(Listen and Acknowledge)**
>
> The next portion of the coaching is about challenges. This is where you get to pick some things you want to work on to make your phone calls even better. **(Make a Statement)**

Was there anything in that call that you think you would have done differently or that you think you could have done better? **(Ask a Question)**

Ask questions to lead agents to self-discovery:

- What do you feel was your greatest challenge on that call?
- What do you think you might have done better?
- If you could change something on that call, what would it be?

This is an application of two more of the principles of positive coaching: Responsibility Rests with Agents and Maintain an Adult Training Environment.

Most agents are used to their coach, manager or supervisor telling them what they did wrong. The positive coach is coming from the perspective that agents are adults and thus fully capable of recognizing the challenges in their own performance.

The positive coach has an important responsibility when agents are identifying their challenges. You must make sure that the challenges can be met by making small changes in agent behavior in a short time. You want agents to recognize that with a few small changes from each week's coaching session, a big change in overall performance will be made over time. This reinforces a point made when setting expectations. You can't do everything at once; instead, work on a few small things at a time and the big picture will improve.

When agents identify and resolve their own challenge, they feel right and smart! Agents will also be more invested in challenges and solutions if it's their idea to work on them.

**When agents identify three challenges, STOP!**

Having agents identify any more than three challenges will turn the session back to the negative. What you want to do is set up your agents for success. Three achievable goals per coaching session are plenty of work. Agents can remain focused on these three challenges; they won't be overwhelmed and will feel confident that they can successfully address them.

# Step Four: Self-Correction

This is may be the most difficult part of the High Five for many of you. In your roles as managers, trainers, and coaches, it's hard to leave the correction to agents. Your experience has given you many solutions and it's easy to share those good ideas; you want to give suggestions or tell agents how to handle situations. The problem is it doesn't work very well.

Does this sound familiar?

> "When I was on the phones, I would _____. You could have done that and the call would have been better."

How many of you remember hearing that from a supervisor?

How many of you wanted to roll your eyes?

That is why it doesn't always work.

Giving answers or suggestions is not the way to true growth and it does not fit in with some of the positive coaching principles, in particular, Responsibility Rests With Agents and Maintain an Adult Learning Environment.

- **Do not** start with suggestions.
- **Do not** tell agents what to fix.
- **Do not** tell agents what to do.

Instead:

- Wait for suggestions from agents.
- Show, tell and guide agents to self-correct.

Use your skill and knowledge to show support for agents. Tell them you know they know how to solve the challenges that they've identified. *Be careful.* This is a point where agents may ask you to give them solutions or suggestions, since they are used to you giving them the answers. Don't do it. If you do, you take responsibility off agents and put it on yourself. Instead, use your LAMA skill to redirect agents to self-correction. Since they are used to being told how to fix something, they may need encouragement to come up with their own solutions.

> The agent asks you:
>
> What do you think I should have said?
>
> The coach's response:
>
> This is great. This is one of the things that I like about the Positive Coach Approach. **(Listen and Acknowledge)**
>
> I know how I would do it. I think that you have good ideas too. You and I may not say it quite the same way. **(Make a Statement)**

What would be the first question you could have asked on this call? **(Ask a Question)**

Ask questions that will encourage agents to self-correct:

- (Name), what might you have done differently?
- What kind of question could you have asked, that may have stimulated the conversation?
- Let's see if we can find a better way to handle that specific situation. Would you like to role-play it with me?

Once agents have picked challenges and come up with ways to self-correct, the next step is to devise a plan to implement the changes.

## Step Five: Personal Performance Plan (Bilateral Action Agreement)

The Personal Performance Plan is a bilateral agreement that you and your agents enter into together. It contains the answers to these four questions:

- What do you want to work on? _____ **(Challenge)**
- What will you do differently to make it happen? _____ **(Self-Correction)**
- How will you remember to work on? _____ **(Challenge from question one)**
- When will you have it done, or learned, or feel good that you will be consistent at it? **(Setting Timelines)**

In steps three and four, you've already answered the first two questions of the plan. The third and fourth questions are usually the hardest for agents to answer. This, in turn, makes it hard for you *not* to provide the answers.

The purpose of question three, asking agents how they will remember to work on a particular challenge, is to make them understand that choosing a path to self-correction is only a start. To enact change, something has to be different; agents must make conscious choices to alter their previous behavior. The easiest way to show this is to give an example.

Let's say that it's always been a requirement for agents to give their names at the start of calls. Some give first and last names and others only give their first name. Management has set a new rule that they must give both first and last names. Even though they know the new rule, agents are forgetful and sometimes only give their first names. This could come up during coaching sessions, with agents and the positive coach both recognizing the error and agents saying that from now on, they will give both names. This is a good start.

Since the agents already knew the rule and are still forgetting to use their last names, you need to get an answer to "How will you remember to give your last name?" This is a tough question and agents may not readily have an answer.

Everyone learns things different ways. Reminders can be vastly different from one agent to the next. Most people learn well with visual reminders; some like to write things down on notepads or sticky notes, and some learn from less common methods. I once trained a woman who used a real Band-Aid® as a symbolic reminder. I wouldn't have used something that symbolic in a million years... but it worked for her.

It's important here for agents to determine what works best for them. The answer to the questions posed to them regarding changing behavior must resonate with them, and not necessarily be what has worked for other agents. That being said, one of the most common reminders used in call centers is the sticky note. This note, placed somewhere visible while actually on calls, is a helpful reminder to be different.

Once you and your agents agree on what type of reminder they will use, you can move onto the last question of the plan: when will it be done or changed or learned? Here, the positive coach will not set the timeline, but instead give a range in which agents can choose their own goals. This is important. It's also important that all challenges be attainable within a week's time. Let agents decide on how many days it will take before the challenge becomes a new habit. This will keep the responsibility on agents and build their confidence.

Write down the answers for each of the three challenges, and give agents a copy of the agreement. You must retain a copy of the agreement as well.

How you end coaching sessions will go a long way toward ensuring their long-term success. Be sure to:

- Summarize all agreements.
- Make sure you each have a copy of the agreements.

- Acknowledge agents for that third thing that you saved for the end of the session, so you can finish on a high note.
- Shake agents' hands and thank them by name.
- Feel good that *you* just had positive coaching session.

**Tip:** Ask agents to come to you for acknowledgment when they achieve their goals. If they're done early, keep a pocket prize handy.

**Caution:** Do not let this tip turn into parental behavior: "I'll be watching you to make sure you do it." This is supposed to be a chance for agents to feel safe to self-acknowledge and for you to have an opportunity to give positive feedback in an informal moment.

# Chapter Nine
# Common Coaching Challenges

You've now learned all the elements of the Positive Coach Approach, and you've been shown how to apply them. We've provided an example of the ultimate coaching session, along with some other resources, at the back of the book. Is this all you need to get started?

Yes and no.

As experienced managers, you've probably run into your share of less-than-cooperative agents. To appropriately handle those situations, you need a bit more in-depth instruction, and we have plenty of experience providing it. We always get "what if" questions during our training sessions with managers—"What if the agent says...?"—so we've developed responses that address the more common scenarios.

The responses we're providing here demonstrate how to use the LAMA Technique to handle the coaching conversation and keep sessions positive, even with agents who don't want to cooperate. The reasons behind these scenarios are psychological.

Since the agents are used to being in an "unsafe environment" it is no surprise that many are defensive and sometimes uncooperative. With practiced use of positive coaching, those situations should not happen often. Because of the positive dialogue that you'll be having with agents, they are less likely to say the things that appear below…but at one time or another, you probably have heard these statements or something quite similar.

Agent responses that create common coaching challenges are:

- "I thought the call was perfect."
- "The customer sounded too busy to buy."
- "I did the best I could."
- "Nobody ever told me that."
- "I don't want to be pushy."
- "I don't know" or "Just tell me."

Let's address how to handle these responses, one by one, using the LAMA Technique.

## "I thought the call was perfect."

Believe it or not, agents won't say this too often, unless the call *was* perfect or close to it. When you do hear this during a coaching session, it is usually said out of fear rather than conceit, as agents typically aren't comfortable self-correcting. They don't feel safe enough to admit error, for fear of being criticized. It's easier for agents to put you on the spot—challenging you to say something negative. Before positive coaching, that was the norm.

Using the LAMA Technique eliminates negative responses, facilitating your ability to support agents' rights to have that opinion. You do not have to make agents wrong…even if the call wasn't perfect.

As part of the coaching process, you will listen to the call again. But first, you must make it safe for agents to hear what transpired. You will use the LAMA Technique as follows:

L - "I thought the call was perfect."

A - "I agree you handled that call well."

M - "I thought I heard at one point the customer sounded uncertain."

A - "Let's listen again and let me know if you hear it, too. Okay?"

Let agents hear what you heard. *Point it out and say...* "This is what I thought I heard…" Provide feedback about what you *thought* you heard. When you present it that way, you create a safe environment. You're not saying you're right and the agent is wrong; instead, you're saying that it is your opinion. By doing that, you make it safe for agents to agree with you about what you *thought* you heard. Try to get agreement from agents about that. You can then role-play, with agents playing the part of the customer.

At this point, if agents still do not agree—denying the feedback— we recommend not pursuing this further. The positive coach will let it go!

Why?

Agents know what you thought you heard. And, you know that they know. If you pursue the issue in the face of their resistance, you'll be making agents wrong. You'll be negating the safe environment and will lose the consultative nature of the session. Agents will think you value their opinions only when they agree with yours.

If this behavior continues to occur, agents may not be at fault. As the coach, you then take responsibility and send them back to training, where they can be provided with the tools to address it.

## "The customer sounded too busy to buy."

This is something you may hear from salespeople and from customer service people who are uncomfortable with sales. Agents may say this when they did not make sales attempts or present offers to serve.

It's human nature to jump to conclusions. When agents assume customers are too busy to buy, they may lose an opportunity to serve the customer fully. Something customers say or do—or even their tone of voice—makes agents assume they are too busy to buy. Our experience tells us otherwise: if it saves customers time, money, or energy, they won't be too busy to buy.

As a positive coach, you want to make agents right and still correct their behavior. What you must do is to teach agents not to jump to that "too busy" conclusion. Make sure agents are clear that what they offer benefits customers. Ask agents to be willing to present benefit information to customers...and let the customer make the decision whether to buy.

You will use the LAMA Technique as follows:

L  – "The customer sounded too busy to buy."

A  – "I understand that you feel that way."

M – "Still, many times our product can be of great value to our customers. They just haven't thought of how it can save them (time, energy or money)."

A  – "To save your customers (time, energy or money), would you be willing to make that offer next time?"

## "I did the best I could."

It's likely you've heard this. Agents look you right in the eye and say…"I did the best I could." It's *so* important to really acknowledge this statement. It's way too easy to make agents wrong, when you really mean to make them feel better.

You've probably said something like: "Oh no, you can do much better than that." You mean to make agents feel good with this statement, but if you look at it carefully, you'll notice it's in complete disagreement with what the agent said! You mean well, but that approach just doesn't work.

What you can say is something that makes agents right! You as the coach need to take full responsibility for agent growth and improvement. Give them the sense that they can do better with training or coaching. If easy changes are required, use coaching sessions to quickly improve performance. If something more involved is appropriate, offer training.

You will use the LAMA Technique as follows for coaching issues:

L - "I did the best I could."

A - "I know you did, and thank you."

M - "I also know that there could be a better way. You have what it takes to be really good at this."

A - "Do you think that we could role-play it now and come up with a way to do it even better?"

You will use the LAMA Technique as follows for training issues:

L - "I did the best I could."

A - "I know you did, and thank you."

M - "I also know that you might do so much better with more training. You have what it takes to be really good."

A - "How about we arrange some training on this so you can learn how to be even more successful?"

## "Nobody ever told me that."

If you hear this statement—and many of you have—you must take it at face value and believe it. Sometimes this is hard to do, but you must give agents the benefit of the doubt. Even if you know agents were in previous classes you taught, and the particular subject was covered, you still must believe them when they say they've never heard it before. In training classes, attendees leave the room, go unconscious and sometimes flat out don't listen.

Acknowledge that you thought it was trained or coached before. Since agents don't always absorb information, you can make them right for saying they haven't heard it before.

Show understanding and offer a solution. Make sure agents learn this item immediately.

Ask agents for agreement to use the newly learned information from now on. This will eliminate agents using this same reason *ever* again on this subject…if you make them right and ask for agreement.

You will use the LAMA Technique as follows:

> L - "Nobody ever told me that."
> A - "I understand. I thought that it *was* in the training but, maybe not."
> M - "I think we can fix this right now."
> A - "If we go over this today, will you use it from now on?"

## "I don't want to be pushy."

This is something you might hear when there are up-sell or cross-sell opportunities. Agents already have initial sales or have handled original customer inquiries; they don't want to press their luck and ask for more, which they equate with being pushy.

It's your job to let them have that feeling and then work on handling it. This may seem difficult, but you are going to make agents right.

You will use the LAMA Technique as follows:

L - "I don't want to be pushy."

A - "I understand. No one wants to seem pushy."

M - "That's why we train: to offer up-sells only when appropriate. We have items that may fit customers' needs."

A - "What do you think you could have offered that would have helped this customer?"

You will follow this LAMA sequence with another that makes agents right for knowing the product to offer and then asks them to offer that item from now on.

## "I don't know." Or, "Just tell me."

The last common coaching challenge is really two in one. First, it's a challenge because agents may be uncomfortable with self-correction, and second, it's a challenge for coaches not to be manipulated into old habits. The old habit we refer to is telling agents how to change or fix the specific challenge from the High Five.

Agents will not always feel safe enough to give input into the self-correction portion of the High Five; they may try to get you to give them the answers. This is what they are used to, and it will seem reasonable to you to help guide them that way. Please don't, unless you truly believe that agents have absolutely no idea how to make specific changes for themselves. Since agents have probably been trained to handle most situations that could have been identified as challenges, they really should know how to self-correct.

Here is a list of things agents may say to get you to give away the answers. Everything on the list can start with either "I don't know" or "Just tell me."

> ...What to say
>
> ...What to do differently
>
> ...What product to offer
>
> ...How to fix it
>
> ...How remind myself
>
> ...How to self-correct

One simple LAMA can handle all of these situations. You will make agents feel right and smart to come up with their own ideas. Then you can discuss how to implement them.

> L - "I don't know how..." or "Just tell me..."
>
> A - "This is a new process. It's not easy learning new things."
>
> M - "I know the answer, but I also know you can think of one as well. You can probably come up with answers that are better for you and in your own words."
>
> A - "What might you have said instead?"

These examples are a good start on how to handle the more common coaching challenges. What you should see by now is a very common thread running through the different LAMA scripts.

Everything starts with making agents right for their feelings. Do not fight them on how they feel; you can never win. Instead, make them right and you can then move on to discovering and implementing solutions. Let agents come up with all the answers. This will take practice on your part, but it will be well worth it.

# Chapter Ten
# Troubleshooting

Just as you need to know how to handle things you might hear from agents, you also must be aware of how to deal with common issues that may come up during the positive coaching process.

## Ten Common Stop Signs

Every company has a list of the most common "stops" on any call. We suggest you make a list of the most common ones and then learn how to engage agents in self-correction. Remember the following things:

- When you need assistance with explaining ideas and supporting agents, use the techniques contained in this book.
- Always model the LAMA Technique when you're coaching.
- Take note that the LAMA Technique is used in every example in this book so you can see the power of positive coaching.
- Make a commitment to use positive coaching every time you attempt to coach or monitor agents.
- You will gain support and improve the performance of both you and your agents when you perform as a positive coach.

We've made our own list of 10 common call "stop signs." We present it below, along with tips on how to address each situation.

# 1. Dead Air

## Monitoring Session Observation:

The customer didn't respond to an agent's question or there was no question posed, resulting in dead air. The agent may have ended on a statement; there may have been implied questions, meaning the agent thought he'd asked something, or the question asked was not one the customer wanted to answer.

## What happens to customers when there is dead air?

When customers don't know how to respond or don't realize that agents want a response, they may feel wrong or stupid to respond, so they say nothing. The resulting dead air is uncomfortable for both customers and agents.

## Coaches' Advice:

Address agents by name and clearly tell them what you heard and observed on the tape. Tell them what you think the solution may be and ask the agent how they would apply this solution.

## Here is how it might sound:

"(Name), you may or may not have realized that you stopped speaking at the end of a statement and left the call path control up to the customer. The solution is always to end on a specific question that will be clearly understood by the customer. Okay? Also, when you end on a question, you are always in control of the conversation. So, what question could you have asked to keep the call along your intended path?"

## 2. Impersonal Attitude

### Monitoring Session Observation:

The customer started with "I am worried," providing reasons for the call before the agent could get the account number. The agent seemed detached and uninterested and asked for the customer's account number without responding to his initial comments.

### What happens to customers in this situation?

Customers may feel that agents aren't  listening, don't care or worse; they often get the impression they're just another caller--or just another number--to agents. Customers can become irate or more irritated because agents don't take their concerns seriously.

### Coaches' Advice:

Address agents by name and clearly tell them you understand the difficulty in hearing the same things over and over all day long. Explain why your suggestion or recommendation will work toward the resolution of the customer's irritation. Ask agents for agreement and ideas from them how they will handle this next time.

**Here is how it might sound:**

"(Name), it must be hard to hear the same things over and over again and still maintain a personal touch. Still, it is important that you show some empathy and understanding. You can do that by using a short acknowledgement phrase before asking customers for their account number. (It sounds like you are concerned. Let's see what we can do to help. What is that account number, please?) Responding with a more personal phrase and acknowledging their worries will keep customers from getting more upset. What words or phrases do you like to use to show empathy before you move the call along by asking for the account number?"

## 3. Call Control and Call Management

**Monitoring Session Observation:**

The customer controls the path of the call and asks questions. The agent responds, but only with answers or statements, and does not ask questions. The agent loses control of the call, finding it difficult to handle an upset customer, move the call along, handle an objection, offer products or determine customer needs. (This example assumes that the agents have been trained in the LAMA Technique for call path control.)

**What happens to customers in this situation?**

Customers have a sense of fear and doubt, and they feel uncertain. They may not know what the next question is or what to do or say. Customers may say they aren't interested because they weren't ever asked a question that made it seem like agents were interested in their needs. Customers will do and say almost anything so as not to appear wrong or stupid.

**Coaches' Advice:**

Address agents by name and clearly explain why call path control is important for them as well as customers. Offer a suggestion or recommendation, giving agents a reason for your solution. Ask agents for a question and encourage them to come up with the answer. Give agents a positive reason to use the LAMA Technique and model it.

**Here is how it might sound:**

"(Name), the LAMA Technique is a way to guide the path of your calls. It's designed to let you lead customers to the end of the call. When you can do this effectively, your communication skills in every facet of your life will be enhanced. You will not hear dead air. Customers will always know what to do next. You will feel a sense of control and ease of speech.  Your job will be more pleasant, because it's always better to be in control, giving customers a feeling of certainty.

The questions are the hardest. What questions could you have used?"

# 4. Customers Don't Get It

**Monitoring Session Observation:**

The customer has to ask the agent to repeat what was just said. The customer doesn't understand the agent. The customer ignores the agent's speech because he didn't hear what the agent said, as the words went by so quickly. The customer gets irritated at the length of the fast talker's information.

**What happens to customers in this situation?**

Customers may feel like they are being tricked or conned when agents talk too fast, and they may not understand what is being said. When agents say too much too quickly, customers may not be able to make decisions. Customers may not purchase just because agents pitched the product or service too fast.

**Coaches' Advice:**

Address agents by name and clearly explain why speaking slowly is important for them as well as customers. Acknowledge agents for being able to speak knowledgably about the product or service. Ask agents if they will listen for customer doubt or wish for a repeat. Encourage agents to slow down. Give them a positive reason to make the change and model the technique they should use. Ask agents how they will fix the problem.

**Here is how it might sound:**

"(Name), the product is no trouble for you, is it? You really know your stuff. And, since you know your product and have given that pitch so often, you may be speaking just a little too fast for some customers. This customer had to ask you to repeat; he may not get it, or he may feel rushed or conned. I suggest you practice a shortened script then say 'okay?' to see if customers get it and are listening to you. Once they agree they are keeping up with you, you can continue on with your pitch. Where do you think would be a good place to slow down and check back with customers?"

## 5. The Positioning of the Price

**Monitoring Session Observation:**

The agent tells the customer of a charge after the customer has agreed to buy and the customer becomes irritated. The agent misrepresents the cost. The product seems free and the customer becomes irritated when told the price in the disclosure. The customer is angry because that cost was not previously disclosed. The customer angrily says, "Why didn't you tell me this earlier? How much is it?"

**What happens to customers in this situation?**

Customers always fear being tricked, conned or over-sold. They don't buy because the price or the cost was delayed to the point of putting doubt in their minds. It's called hedging on the price. Customers resent having to wait for the price as if there was some secret about it. They make many decisions based on price.

**Coaches' Advice:**

Address agents by name and clearly explain why the money issue is so important for them as well as customers. Offer a suggestion or recommendation, giving agents a reason for your solution. Ask agents for a question and encourage them to come up with the answer.

**Here is how it might sound:**

"(Name), the best way to offer a price is to provide it after you have given customers a feature and a benefit...before it's too late. Let's put the money in strategically between two other things. That way, customers know what they are buying, but they aren't asked to buy until they have enough information to decide. What will you say to present the feature, the benefits, and the cost earlier in the call?"

# 6. Persistence Can Be Pushy

**Monitoring Session Observation:**

The customer becomes irritated because the agent will not give up. The agent acts like he won't take no for an answer and the customer sounds disgusted. The agent uses a question that appears to have a threat in it. "Don't you want to protect your credit?" The customer has to say no thanks or such three times.

**What happens to customers in this situation?**

Customers think your company is into selling stuff they don't need. They get worried and don't feel it's "safe" to call the company. They may never call you again, which means you won't be able to sell them the next product. Customers feel pressed or threatened and therefore lash out at agents.

**Coaches' Advice:**

Address agents by name and clearly explain why there is a fine line between being persistent and pushy, and it's important for them and customers to understand that. Then ask them what they can say to not sound or feel pushy next time.

**Here is how it might sound:**

"(Name), I may have confused you when I asked you to handle objections. I don't mean that you should be pushy. I suggest you use the LAMA Technique. Offer customers features and benefits two times. If they refuse the second time, go ahead and complete the call. You don't need to push after you have received two noes; not everyone is willing to buy today. What could you say after getting turned down that would not feel pushy and invite the customer to buy in the future?"

## 7. Requirement—A Second Attempt

**Monitoring Session Observation:**

The agent offered the product or service once, but did not make a second attempt. The agent made the attempt by reading a script and asking for the order, but when told no, he gave up and said goodbye. The agent quit too soon and only briefly described the product or service.

**What happens to customers in this situation?**

Customers may be happy that no further sales message came. However, customers may need the product or service, but since they weren't provided with all the features or benefits, they couldn't make an informed choice.

Customers may feel you had a product or service that you didn't give them a chance to find out about and buy. The free trial period may have worked perfectly here.

**Coaches' Advice:**

Address agents by name and make sure they understand your faith in them. Ask them to role-play to get them a little more comfortable when making that second attempt. Give agents a positive reason to use the LAMA Technique and model it. Ask them to try it on their next call.

**Here is how it might sound:**

"(Name), I count on the fact that you always ask for the order. And at the same time, I did not hear a second attempt. It is a little risky to go for the second attempt. I do understand. However, the first time customers say no, they often mean *I don't know enough about it to choose*. Or, they may have thought they weren't interested because you didn't happen to hit their hot button in your first sentence. Please make it your goal to make two attempts to sell. Let's figure out how you are comfortable making the attempt and when you come up with a good way you'll use it. Okay?"

## 8. An Opportunity Missed

**Monitoring Session Observation:**

The agent didn't make any attempt at the cross-selling opportunity. He decided not to make the offer at all, even though there was a clear "buying signal." The customer ended the call abruptly, so the agent had no chance to make the offer. The requirements have already been met for attempts today.

## What happens to customers in this situation?

If no offer is made, customers may not be aware of a product or service they may need. Customers may not think there is a way to save money with your product or service, they may want the peace of mind they would enjoy with the product or service, or they may wish to know about all the products and services your company offers. Customers want help, but agents don't know this because no attempt is made.

## Coaches' Advice:

Address agents by name and clearly explain why hearing a buying signal and making an attempt is important for them as well as customers. Customers make decisions on the information we provide. Ask agents to give up their judgments and come up with a way to make the cross-sell.

## Here is how it might sound:

"(Name), the best way to make sure that you have great stats and customers are completely served is to give up your judgments. Do not decide which customer might need our services. Instead, offer the services and let the customer decide. You will increase your sales, making you more money, and you will be sure that customers who need the service have had the opportunity to buy. Right? I know that you do this easily when customers are pleased with you. What can you do to remind yourself to give up your judgments and simply make an attempt on every call even when you don't have the most cooperative customer?"

# 9. When "Is there anything else I can do for you?" Doesn't Work

**Monitoring Session Observation:**

The customer was not prepared for a cross-sell. The customer thought the call was over and started to hang up. The agent seemed to be scrambling to bring the attention of the customer back to the cross-sell opportunity. The call seemed over in every way.

**What happens to customers in this situation?**

When agents appear to end calls by asking if customers have any more questions, customers think the call is over if they have no more questions. Customers will feel that when agents continue, their time is being used without their consent. Customers think their business is completed, so why go on?

**Coaches' Advice:**

Address agents by name and clearly explain that why and when you ask customers if they have any questions is important, both for them and their customers.

**Here is how it might sound:**

"(Name), you did the customer service side of the call so well that the customer felt completely taken care of. That is a good thing. However, most customers know that the 'Is there anything else I can do for you?' is really the dismissal question. So you want to make a transition to your cross sell before asking that question.

Let's figure out a good transition over to the cross-sell and then you can do it his new way and save the 'anything else' for the real end of the call. Okay?"

## 10. Customers Want Certainty

**Monitoring Session Observation:**

No acknowledgment was given to the customer at the end of the call. You didn't hear any type of closing statement: "You will really love this service." "You did the right thing by getting this service. It will save you money." "You can call us anytime and we will always help you. I am glad you called today." "It was a pleasure to talk with you today."

**What happens to customers in this situation?**

Customers like to have someone tell them they did the right thing to call. Customers want to know they made the right choice to call, complain, ask questions or buy services. They think you are there to serve them and they like to know that you are happy to do it. Customers expect you to be happy to take care of them; they like to be acknowledged.

**Coaches' Advice:**

Address agents by name and clearly explain why certainty is important for them as well as customers. Ask agents how they prefer to give this acknowledgement.

**Here is how it might sound:**

"(Name), you always are so polite at the end of your calls (or you really handled that ending and wrap up well). May I recommend that you say one more thing at the end of calls that will give you an 'exceeding customer's expectation.'

Say a closing statement, like one of these: 'You can call us anytime; we are always glad to help. It's our job.' 'You did the right thing by trying out that product.' 'You are really going to like this service and it will save you money, too.' What are the words you would use to make the customer feel smart and right to have called us?"

**Troubleshooting Wrap-up**

Take these examples and work with them to fit your specific needs. We provide them to plant the seed with you. There are many ways you can handle these stop signs and make them your own. In many of these examples, you will see that the coach expects the agent come up with his own solution or his own words to handle the customer.

We believe that after applying the concepts and methods presented in this book, you will come up with the way that works best for you. Take the Positive Coach Approach and make it your own. Follow the guidelines; your agents will receive you better and their performance will show marked improvement.

# Chapter Eleven
# Getting Started

## Getting Started

You now have all the ideas, theories, tools and skills to get started with the Positive Coach Approach. Wondering what to do next?

We've come up with some ideas on how to best implement the Positive Coach Approach (PCA) in your call center. Like the agents that you'll coach, you'll need a plan. Yours will be two-fold: how to make the time for positive coaching and how to improve your own coaching skills once you begin using the PCA.

## Make Time for Coaching

First:

- Start your walk-by coaching.
- Acknowledge at least one agent per day with public and positive feedback.
- Set up timelines; work coaching into your schedule.

By giving positive feedback, you will start to create a safe environment for your agents.

Next:

- Begin using the PCA in your coaching sessions.
- Coach at least two agents per week. (One a day is recommended for the first two weeks.)
- Be sure to start all your sessions by explaining what positive coaching is and how it will be different for both you and agents.

You may find yourself challenged in the early going, but once you make positive coaching a part of your regular routine, you'll wonder how you ever got along without it.

## Improve Your Own Coaching Skills

It's very important to enhance your coaching skills as you continue using the PCA with your agents. As you would expect, we have some suggestions on how to do that:

- Dedicate time to review your performance at least once a week.
- If there are multiple coaches in your organization utilizing the PCA, work with each other on your coaching skills.
- Secure permission from one or two agents to record their coaching sessions, letting them know that you'll be reviewing the recordings to improve your own (positive coaching) skills.
- Listen to the recordings and take yourself through the High Five. Be sure to use all five steps, as you would with agents.

# Self-Coach Using the High Five

Set expectations for your coaching performance.

- I will use the LAMA Technique and ask questions.
- I will not give advice or answers.
- I will follow the High Five.
- I will give specific and complete acknowledgments.

Acknowledge yourself…and be specific.

- I used good questions that made it easy for Jim to self acknowledge.
- "What was your favorite part of the call" worked great on Bill.
- I started to say what I used to do for XYZ and then stopped and asked Kelly how she would like to do XYZ. (That was hard, but I did it!)

### Find Challenges

- Jenny asked for my idea and I told her before I asked her opinion. She said she would do it "my way." That's not where I wanted to go on that one.
- Bob was so hard on himself that I told him to "shake it off." I didn't acknowledge his feelings. I moved on without letting him know it was okay to feel that way and it is fine as long as he can come up with a solution for the next time.

### Self-Correct and Make a Plan

- I'll put a note on my coaching form that says, "Don't tell! Ask for ideas."
- I'll give myself three coaching sessions to stop giving away the answers.

- I won't expect others to "shake it off" just because I can do that.
- I'll put a reminder on my form that says, "You are right to feel that way..."
- I'll give myself six positive coaching sessions to use the "feel right" phrase.

It's very important to remember that it will take time and practice to apply this process skillfully and in the manner it was intended. The ideas behind the Positive Coach Approach make good sense and the skills within it are just that, skills. Practice and *positive self-coaching* will make you a master!

## Praising is Required

Positive coaching is all about making agents feel right and smart. For that reason, you need to be aware of the numerous opportunities to praise agents. Some are listed here:

Praise agents when they:

- Take personal interest in customers
- Make customers feel right and smart to use your company
- Control and guide call paths
- Know product features and benefits
- Make features and benefits fit customer needs
- Perform a perfect transition
- Attempt sales twice
- Close with certainty

- Complete disclosure perfectly
- Use customers' names three times per call
- Keep customers for life

Your praise may be verbal (way to go!) or you may hand out small tokens of appreciation. Everyone likes a free lunch now and then.

## Positive Coaching—An Overview

You've learned a lot in this book; we know it's a lot to take in. Here's a synopsis of how to use positive coaching to ensure your agents are the best they be and have the chance to grow in a safe environment.

- Use a form. Show agents the form you will be using during coaching sessions.
- List expectations. Tell agents what you are looking for.
- Listen to three calls. Listen with agents.
- Pick out three acknowledgements. Choose three things agents did well and acknowledge during coaching sessions.
- Focus on the positives. Spend as much time or more on what your agents do well as you do on correcting errors.
- Tell agent two of the acknowledgements. Save one for the session end.
- Use the LAMA Technique. Demonstrate it repeatedly.
- Ask questions. "What do you think was the best part of the call? What else?"
- Ask agents what they want to improve on? List two-three items.
- Ask agents how they will do it? Get agents to explain their plans.

- Show, tell and guide. Use role-playing, demonstrate the behavior and explain how to do it.

- Ask agents when improvement will occur. Obtain a timeline, within one week.

- Write agreements. Prepare a list together that includes what agents have agreed to do.

- Determine when the next session will occur. Set an appointment.

- Use the "saved" acknowledgement. End the session with a compliment.

Both you and your agents should file a copy of the acknowledgements list for future reference. It's a good idea to provide agents with a journal where they can record thoughts from coaching sessions and items on which they wish to improve.

## The Coaches' Pledge

Never stray from your mission of being a positive coach. Here's a pledge you should keep handy.

- I promise to talk to every member of my team at least once a day.

- I promise to have a huddle coaching briefing two times a month to support agents' individual goals and keep their sales skills in tiptop shape.

- I promise to catch 'em doing something right by walking onto their playing field specifically to give positive feedback.

- I promise not to use negative or parental tactics with anyone in my charge.

- I expect championship performance from my team… nothing less than their very best at all times.

# Appendix A
# The Ultimate Coaching Session

Let's look at how a Positive Coach Approach session would go if all lessons in this book were applied in a single session.

Diane will do several things throughout the conversation. The lessons are found in the Four Foundational Imperatives.

## Imperative One: Four Building Blocks

*Intention* - to create a Safe Environment,

*Relationship* - Always make the agent feel Right and Smart to work with the Coach,

*Discipline* (Self-discipline) - Practice all skills and ideas, and

*Skill* - Use LAMA technique throughout the conversation.

## Imperative Two: The LAMA Technique

*Listen, Acknowledge, Make a statement, and Ask a question.* The use of this technique makes the meeting conversational and consultative.

## Imperative Three: Eight Guiding Principles

- Create and Maintain a Safe Environment
- Create a Consultative Environment
- Build Self-Esteem by Focusing on the Positives
- Maintain an Adult Training Environment
- The Responsibility to Learn and Grow Lies with Agents
- Timelines are Essential
- Use Bilateral Action Agreements
- Questions are the Key

## Imperative Four: The High Five Method

1. Expectations
2. Acknowledgments
3. Challenges
4. Self-Correction
5. Personal Performance Plan

What is actually happening is all the lessons are intertwined. In the column on the left I will point out which of these lessons is identifiable at that point in the conversation. Diane uses the LAMA technique every time she speaks. Diane is constantly applying the other elements as well.

First let's set the physical stage.

Diane is the coach and Mark is the telephone sales rep. Diane is a Supervisor and has occasional contact with Mark. Mark has been inside Diane's office before today and it is usually not for praise. Most of their private meetings have been yearly reviews, a couple of "Atta Boys", and an occasional reprimand. This is the norm of their contact to date.

This is an "Unsafe Environment" for Mark. Like many people he is wary of *any* contact with his supervisor.

At this point Diane is going to use her office for a coaching session and Mark will have some misgivings about how this will be different from a reprimand. He may be thinking "Oh yeah, this is just another chance to be told that I am doing something wrong, AGAIN". This is how most "coaching" or "monitoring" is perceived.

Diane is a Positive Coach.

She will have her agenda in mind and invite Mark into her office. I will next go through the coaching session as if we were listening to the conversation. Then, I will tell you what the Positive Coach did that was different and why Diane did those things.

Diane *intends* to *create a safe environment*. By putting Mark at ease.

Diane " Good morning Mark. We are going to do something a little different today. I recently learned a new coaching technique called the Positive Coach Approach. It is very different from how we've talked about your calls in the past and I am looking forward to trying my newly learned skills."

Sitting next to each other is less intimidating therefore, a *safe environment* for Mark.

Diane sits and offers Mark a seat on the same side of the desk.

*Safe environment, Consultative environment*

Diane says "I have a format to this new coaching and I think that you will like it too. It is set up to be positive, and for both of us to participate in each step of the process. Let me show you the form, okay?"

Mark "Okay."

*Safe environment*

Diane shows the Positive Coach Approach form.

*Questions are the key*

Diane " Now, this form is meant as a record of this session. Mark, I want to be clear that it will only be used as a tool for this meeting only and does not go into any permanent file except as a record of what we talk about. We will be doing these sessions regularly and may not ever need to refer to these forms again. I will also make sure that you get a copy of this after each meeting too. Any questions so far?"

*LAMA technique.* Notice all four steps

*Mark is still a little unsafe.*

Mark "If you're not going to use this later, why do you need to keep it?"

*Builds self-esteem and confidence*

Diane " That's a good question. As your skills improve, we may want to look back on the things that you have worked on and changed and talk about them. This form is really used as a reference tool mostly. Let's get started, okay?"

Mark "Okay."

**First step of High Five:**
*Expectations*

Diane "First of all we are going to pick three things that we both expect to happen on each call. Since we haven't done this before I will start off and pick two items and you can pick the third, okay?"

*Consultative*

Mark "Sure."

Diane "Good. On each Sales call we can expect to hear you identify yourself and the company clearly at the outset, right?"

*Questions are key*

Mark "Yes"

Diane "Alright, secondly on almost every call you will have the opportunity to ask for the sale, right?"

*Questions are key*

Mark "Well, not on every call. Some callers only want information."

*Relationship* - Make agent right

Diane "You are right! Some callers are set on not buying today. So, let's listen to see if the opportunity was there then did you ask for the sale. Okay Mark, what would you like the third expectation to be?"

*Consultative*

Mark "Umm, how about..Did I answer all the customer's questions correctly."

*Safe environment*

Diane "Good, so we'll put down gave correct information. Next we will listen to the call. Let me tell you this is where this really gets different. We are going to listen to

*Consultative*

the call together. I have not listened to this call yet. As a matter of fact, we have all of yesterday's calls recorded why don't you pick the call off the computer to listen to. Any call that lasts 2-3 minutes would probably be a good call for coaching. Which call do you want to listen to?"

Mark "I get to pick?"

*Positive/Builds Confidence*

*Responsibility Rests with the Agent*

Diane "Sure, let's set you up for success. Did you feel that you had your best calls in the morning or afternoon?"

Mark "I was doing good after lunch. Any one of those will do. I think I had a really good call around 2:00."

*A short LAMA*

Diane "Okay, I see a 3 minute call at 1:42. Is that one okay?"

Mark "Sure."

*Adult training environment*

*Responsibility rests with the agent*

Diane "As I said Mark, this is a little different. While we are listening to the call I would like you to notice all the things that you do well... I know it is easier to pick out the negatives and we will talk about those too. After we listen, we are going to spend time on the good stuff. But, what makes this positive, is listening for what you do right every day. Okay, let's listen".

Diane and Mark listen to the recorded call.

Step Two of High Five:
*Acknowledgments*

*Questions are key*

*Positive/Builds Confidence*

*Questions are key*

*LAMA technique*

*Positive/Builds Confidence.*

Diane "Well Mark, I heard a lot of good things on that call. First off, you gave your name and the company name slowly and clearly so that the customer knew exactly who she was talking to. I also heard you use the customer's name at least 4 times. I know that we generally ask for 3 per call and you exceeded that and I could hear that the customer really liked that you called her Mrs. Johnson. She sounded elderly and you and I both know that that generation appreciates the formality. What did you like most about that call?"

Mark "Well, I did use her name and I could hear that she was older. But, I thought that I could have pushed harder on the upsell?"

Diane "Well that may be true. What I heard was that you did, at least, offer the upsell. Not everyone is comfortable even making that offer. I thought that you making the offer was great. What else did you think that you did well on?"

Mark "I don't know, it was just a regular call."

Diane "Yes it was. There is so much that you do right every day that it seems "regular" and each of those things are things that you had to learn to do and then you applied that learning. Before we move on, why don't you pick out another thing that you did well. What would

*Consultative*

you say that your favorite part of the call was?"

Mark "My favorite part...I guess it was answering her questions enough to know that she was ready to buy and then making the sales offer."

*Responsibility rests with agents*

Diane "YES! I agree. **You** identified that she was ready to buy and then you made your offer and then **you** made the attempt at the upsell as well. Thank you that is exactly how it should be done! What else did you like?"

*Positive/ Builds Confidence*

Mark "I don't know, I do know what I should have done."

*Positive/Builds Confidence*

Diane "Okay, well I think we both identified several things that you did really well on that call. Let's move on to the challenges. What would you say you would like to have done differently?"

*Step Three of the High Five: Challenges*

Mark "I think that I should have probed more on her needs. If I did, I may have succeeded with that upsell attempt."

*Responsibility rests with the agent*

Diane "Sure, the more you know about the customer, the easier it is to tailor the presentation to fit their needs. You are right. I heard you ask a few questions. And you did get the sale. What question or questions do you think that you could have asked?"

*LAMA Technique*

*Responsibility rests with the agent*

Mark "I should have probed further since we offer up sells based on information the customer provides."

**Step Four of the High Five:** *Self Correction*

Diane "Okay, good. I know we have some standard questions that we use to gather information so that the upsell will be a good fit. Which question do you like to start out with?"

This can get tricky. Coaches please, don't give away the answer.

Mark "I don't know. I use different questions each time, depending on the situation. What do you think I should have said?"

*Positive/Builds Confidence*

Diane "This is great. This is one of the things that I like about the Positive Coach Approach. I know how I would do it. I think that you have good ideas too. You and I may not say it quite the same way. What would be the first question you could have asked on this call?"

*Responsibility rests with the agent*

Mark "Oh I see you're going to make me come up with the answer..."

**Step Four of the High Five:** *Self Correction*

Diane "Exactly right, each of us has our own way and we can both get there on different paths. I want you to choose the question that is easiest for you to use. So what would you ask first?"

Mark "Okay, when someone sounds older I would say...We have some great offers that benefit different age groups. May I ask, which age group do you fit in? 30-45, 45-60 or 60 plus?"

Step Five of the High Five: *Personal Performance Plan*

Diane "Perfect. That sets you right on the road to offer that upsell. Now, here's the hard part... How are you going to remember to ask that question the next time a similar situation comes up? Do you need a reminder?"

Mark " I don't know what you mean by reminder. I think that I will just do it."

*Responsibility rests with the agent*

Diane "Let me be more clear. When you want to add something new that doesn't happen naturally, like asking the age range, you need to have some sort of trigger to remind yourself to be different. What works for you when you want to add something new?"

*Questions are key*

Mark "Oh, I see. When we first started giving first and last names I used a sticky note that said LAST NAME."

*Positive/Builds Confidence*

Diane "That is exactly what I mean. Do you think a note like that will work here?"

Mark "Yes, sure."

*Time lines are essential*

Diane "Great. Now here is the next question...How many days will it take before you are comfortable that the age range question will be as natural as giving your last name?"

Mark "Wow, that's tough."

*Adult training environment*

Diane "Yes, this is getting down to the nitty gritty. Okay let's look

*Positive/Builds Confidence*

at it this way. I know that you can get this done in a week or less. It only took you one full day to get used to saying your last name. With concentration on your reminder, when within a weeks time will you have this done?"

Mark "Okay. I think it will take me five days."

*Responsibility rests with the agent*

*Bilateral action agreement*

*Positive/Builds Confidence*

Diane "That's great Mark. Five days is a reasonable goal and I think that this is a done deal. Thank you. You have done a lot of work in this session and I want to thank you for all your input. One more thing before you go. There was a moment on that call where you really took the time to thank that customer for her business. You had already made the sale and you did not have to go further, but you did. I think that that extra after a sale really keeps the customers happy and it creates great word of mouth. Good job Mark! Thanks"

*Safe environment*

Diane shakes Marks hand and walks him out.

# Appendix B
# The Power of Questions

Throughout this book, we have stressed the importance of asking questions as an important component of positive coaching. You've already been provided with a number of examples of that, but since there are many different types of questions coaches can ask, we've dedicated this section to looking at some different types of questions and identifying how to use them effectively. Remember, the person asking the questions is the person in control of the conversation.

There are open-ended, closed-ended and alternate choice questions and each has a specific use in the LAMA Technique. The secret of the technique is in the way the questions are set up at the end of the four-step process. By using an acknowledgment and a statement in front of any question, it becomes less intrusive. Questions then take on a power of their own, which can guide the conversation in the direction the coach chooses.

Use questions to:

- Control the conversation in general
- Set up agents for a response
- Set up the next subject to be discussed
- Show interest in the person being coached (If you want to be interesting to someone, act interested in them!)

- Open the door to a new topic
- Ask for input
- Ask for agreement
- Inquire about anything

## Open-Ended Questions

Open-ended questions encourage explanation and promote dialogue. This type of question works best when it begins with what or how. It's commonly used in opening statements, probing situations and handling objections.

Some examples are:

- What part of the call did you like best?
- How will you handle a similar situation next time?
- How did you feel about the customer's response?
- What do you think you could have done differently?
- What else did you like about that call?
- Where would you like to be this time next year?
- What caused you to make that decision?

Each one of these open-ended questions encourages agents to talk. This is exactly what the coach wants, because it's critical in the coaching process to provide agents with the opportunity to speak and be listened to. This works to maintain the safe environment and promote self-discovery.

# Closed-Ended Questions

Closed-ended questions can usually be answered with a simple statement of fact, or a yes or no; they do not promote dialogue. These questions usually begin with have you, how many, how much, etc. These type of questions are typically used in summarization and wrap-up. You will also use them in the final stage of the High Five Method, when you and your agents will be making an action plan.

Some examples are:

- How many calls do you usually take during a day?
- How long have you been on this project?
- When were you last coached?
- Is there anything else you would like to work on?
- Would you like to know more about it?
- Have I explained that clearly?
- Is that what you had in mind?
- Would that work for you?
- How does that sound?
- When will you have that accomplished?
- What day would work best for you?
- When shall we meet again?

It seems that with most people, the tendency is to use closed-ended questions because they usually evoke the most direct answer. Coaches habitually use closed-ended questions the most because they require only a short answer and no conversation...but this is counterproductive to the positive coaching process. It is very important to pay attention to the type of question used.

**The quality of the question counts.**

## Alternate Choice Questions

Alternate choice questions can be used effectively to give agents being coached a feeling of empowerment. As the name suggests, this type of question is used to give agents a choice. It is also used as a tool to narrow down the options offered during the coaching process. Alternate choice questions prevent coaches from making limits sound like ultimatums.

**Example:**

Avoid asking: "How many days would you like to meet this target?"

Instead, ask:  "Bill, I think you can get this done by either Friday or Monday. Which would you prefer?"

**Explanation:**

This method provides a "this or that" alternative and makes the process seem friendlier, while still giving agents the indication that they have the responsibility to see the change accomplished by a target date.

Other examples are:

- Would next week work for you, or would you prefer the end of this week?

- We could coach again next Monday or would tomorrow work better for you?

- Would you prefer coaching here at your desk or somewhere more private?

Tip: It's better for coaches to give the choice they prefer last. This the key to a good alternate choice question. Agents will often pick the last choice they heard. This will work great as a sales tool, too. Have your agents try this with customers as well!

## Avoid Intrusive Questions

Questions that start with "why" are very often construed as intrusive. Coaches who are looking for justification of agent actions may be asking these types of questions. Intrusive questions may make agents feel wrong or stupid and will often receive less-than-cheerful responses. Coaches may think that happens because agents are defensive, but in reality it's because a poor question was asked.

Make a list of the questions coaches use on a regular basis. Listen to the phrasing and the context. Questions such as, "Why didn't you use the customer's name three times on that call?" can be so irritating to agents that when they answer, they become defensive and angry.

### Example:

Don't ask, "Why did you give *that* answer to the customer?" Instead, say, "Let me ask, what was your thinking behind giving that answer to your customer?"

### Explanation:

The first question is intrusive, and it also sounds as if it is a forgone conclusion that the answer was wrong. The second question implies nothing is wrong and only makes the offer to discuss the agent's decision.

Use the LAMA Technique with this type of probing to soften the question. Then, add a good question that won't cause agents to become irritated and you have a more congenial conversation.

## Make a List

It is wise to make a list of questions that work to satisfy your objectives and help you start coaching conversations. You might think you already know how to ask questions, but if you notice, you'll find most of your questions may be closed-ended or direct, like those mentioned above. Conversational questions will help move coaching sessions to the next step.

To ask a conversational question, begin with "what" or "how." Check to see if those questions promote conversation. For example "What time do you want to begin coaching?" will not work. Take your time and see how many conversational questions you can write. Pick out the 10 best and make a list. Refer to this list whenever you need to, to keep conversations open.

Consider the following examples:

- What caused you to make that decision?
- What were the circumstances that...?
- How can I be of assistance?
- What was the best part of the call?
- What would you do to improve?
- What would you change?
- How did the call go for you?

- When the customer said _____, what did you think about that?
- When the dead air happened, what happened just before that?
- How will you remember to learn it?
- What will you do to remind yourself to practice?
- How can I help you fix it?
- What do you think would work to fix that situation?
- What could you have done to make the customer feel better about it?
- Was there anything that you might have done to close the call sooner?
- How knowledgeable was the customer?

## Preface Questions With Transitional Phrases

What if agents don't give you the chance to ask any questions? In these instances, we suggest using a bridge or transitional phrase to set up the following question. A bridge explains why the coach is asking a question and includes a statement that softens it. In addition, the bridge could include a permission to ask additional probing questions. Using a bridge or transitional phrase before a question sets up agents to expect a question and thereby lowers the resistance to answering them.

Consider these examples:

**Example:**

"I know it is hard to self-acknowledge and it is unusual. This is the way coaching will be from now on and I really want you to be able to recognize what you do well and acknowledge yourself for it. So tell me, what did you like most about that call?"

**Explanation:**

Use a transitional phrase to put the agent at ease and then ask a question.

**Example:**

The next portion of the coaching is about challenges. This is where you get to pick some things that you want to work on to make your phone calls even better. Was there anything in that call that you think you would have done differently or that you think you could have done better?

**Explanation:**

Use a transitional phrase to change the subject, followed by a question that begins the new subject.

**Example:**

"I now want to ask you several questions that will help us develop an agreement on how you plan to improve. The first question is, what part of the call do you want to work on?"

**Explanation:**

Set up a series of questions by telling agents that there are more questions to come. This will make this part of the process seem less like an interrogation and make it more comfortable for agents to answer the questions.

It's always a good idea to write out transitional phrases.

## Make Your Coaching Sessions About Agents

You should always focus on agents during your coaching sessions, whether you are making statements or asking questions. This is key to having effective coaching sessions. This means that every phrase and nuance of your tone should stress the benefits of positive coaching. Agents want to hear what's in it for them.

And remember…follow every statement with a question! Questions are the key!

# Appendix C
# Kenny and the Coach

## by Judy McKee

After I completed a training session with a very large corporation, I was walking through the call center on my way to work with the coaches. As I was passing by a manager's desk, she asked me to stop a minute and give her some tips on coaching. I was flattered and I asked her what kinds of problems was she having.

The manager said she had a man in her group named Kenny who she thought ought to be doing well selling his product, which was a subscription to a  national sports magazine. His job was to turn customer inquiries into sold subscriptions. He was not doing well; he was about to be let go since his numbers were so low. He was losing his self-esteem and she was perplexed, since she felt he had potential when she hired him.

Kenny was really struggling and she had tried coaching him several times, offering solutions to him on how he might do better, but he didn't seem to "catch on" to her ideas. She had offered help, threatened him and finally had given up. She just didn't know what else to do.

I looked over at Kenny from where her desk was and he looked like an intelligent human being, so I asked the manager a couple of questions. The first questions were, "Does Kenny have a family?" and "Does Kenny drive a car?" She said he had a family and he did have a car. I said, if Kenny can drive a car and bring up a family, he can easily learn to sell this magazine.

I noted that selling this product was not hard, not brain surgery or rocket science. It required a two-minute phone call and was a great product. Selling has rules and if he followed the rules, he would succeed. The manager said she thought so, too, but Kenny just wasn't producing the way that was required of him. I asked her if she had faith in him and believed in him. She said she used to, but now she was just not able to back up her belief in him. I said maybe Kenny can feel your lack of confidence in him and he just needs sincere encouragement in a "safe environment."

That's when she asked me to talk to him. I felt a little funny doing that, because I hadn't trained him and he might not feel safe with a stranger, but I went over to Kenny and asked him if I could have the honor of coaching him even though I had not trained him. I told him I was working with his manager to show her how to coach and I needed him as someone to help me demonstrate my positive coaching techniques. He said he would be happy to let me coach him.

As I sat down in the chair next to him and got the phone jack hooked up and the headset in my ear, I noticed he had many pictures on the wall of his wife, his boat, his car and his kids. I immediately identified him as a hard-working family man with a steady, stable personality. I knew that he wanted certainty and confidence and would do what it takes to get the job done. I asked Kenny the names of the kids and his wife and his boat. He gave me the information and then asked him how he liked the products of the company and did he think he was selling as well as he could? He said he loved the product and the company, but he thought he could do better in the number of sales he made.

I asked him to make a couple calls. I also asked him if he would like me to make any recommendations, since I had been in the sales training business for 20 years. He said he would be glad for any good ideas that I may have. I listened to two quick calls and stopped him. I noticed that he needed some work in asking questions. He was very helpful answering customer queries, but he didn't feel comfortable or maybe he was never taught to take control of the conversation.

It was at this time I realized he needed a confidence builder and a way to talk that make him comfortable asking questions. He needed some simple selling skills; that would make all the difference. I used my Positive Coach Approach with him and showed the manager how to use it at the same time.

I started by telling Kenny what I thought was great on the calls. I gave him some specifics on exactly what he did well. He brightened up immediately and seemed to have no fear of me. Next, I asked him what he thought went well and he named a few things, too. Then, his manager started to interrupt him with some comments about what went wrong on the calls and I stopped her in mid-sentence.

I asked Kenny to tell me what he thought needed to work on, and he commented on what he could do to make his calls better. I gave him a high five and said, "Fantastic! You can self-correct."

I continued by asking Kenny to come up with some questions to ask customers that would help them make a decision. He wrote down a couple questions and I asked him to make a call and use the questions. It was at this point that I gave him a trial close question to use if he thought it was appropriate. He took another call and sold a subscription; then, he did it again.

At this point I gave him another high five and said he should write all this down and set new goals. Anyone who can raise a beautiful family like he had, drive a car and learn so quickly how to ask questions could be the top producer around here. He just beamed, his manager beamed, and I knew when I left them, they had a new and wonderful relationship to reestablish. Kenny had some confidence in himself.

After the session, I spoke with his manager again. I told her that this product was easy to sell, and Kenny could easily do this job. I asked her to have more faith in Kenny and also to stop helping him, but give Kenny confidence in himself by allowing him to self-correct. I suggested using the positive coaching theory of adult education principles by helping Kenny to help himself.

Over the next several weeks, Kenny continued to self-correct and made much higher numbers. Everybody was happier. The manager did not have to be parental. Kenny could use his own ideas and intelligence for his own success. The company reaped the rewards.

These are the rewards you can have by using the Positive Coach Approach.

# Appendix D
# McKee Motivation Positive Coach Approach Form

McKee Motivation – Phonedamentals          The Positive Coach Approach©

## Positive Coach Approach©

### Format for PCA Coaching Session

Directions for form

## Expectations
Set expectations for each coaching session before listening to calls. Pick two or three things to listen for. You may pick items from the agent's last coaching session "challenges" section or you may pick from your own list of expectations

## Listen to the call all the way through.

## Acknowledgements
1. Listen for the things that you heard that went well on the call, write down three of them. Be sure to find at least three. Keep notes so that you can be specific with the agent.
   - Examples are often chosen from the "expectations" list. Or other QA lists.

### Coach Acknowledges First

2. The coach acknowledges the agent for two of the three items *be specific*. Save the third for the end of the session.

3. Ask the agent to acknowledge him/her self. Use The LAMA to prompt the agent to do this. (At this point the agent may want to go negative. Acknowledge that and let them know that first you are going to talk about all the positives). Acknowledge each thing they say and ask them to keep going until they can think of no more acknowledgements.

The next three steps of the High Five Method will actually be done for each separate challenge.

## Challenges

1. Notice up to three specific challenges that the agent may want to work on from this call. (Pick only three. You may or may not need these later.)

### Agent Chooses Challenges First

2. Ask the agent what they would like to work on from this call or if it is a really good call what they would like to make their challenge for this coaching session.
    - You may need to help the agent define the challenge so that it will be an attainable goal. You can do this by using the LAMA technique to have their agreement on the definition.
3. If the agent cannot come up with challenges you may use your notes to define the challenges for this session. CAUTION: Do not suggest to them what to fix.
    - Tell them what you thought you heard and ask if they heard it too. Once you have that agreement, ask if that could be one of their challenges this week. Use LAMA to do this.

## Self-Correction

Using the LAMA work with the agent to discover.
What will the agent do differently to correct the chosen challenge?
How will the agent remember to do that thing differently?
Ex. The agent may put up a post it on their monitor with a reminder of some kind.
CAUTION: Do not suggest to them how to make this change.

## Personal Performance Plan

Using the LAMA ask the agent to set a timeline to correct this challenge.
When will the agent have this done?
Let the agent know that they may pick the timeline. Also, let them know that they are good enough to complete any challenge in as little as one day to one week.

McKee Motivation – Phonedamentals                The Positive Coach Approach©

# Positive Coaching Form

Name: _____ Date: _____ Coach: _____

## Expectations:
Name three things to listen for on this call.

_____

_____

**LAMA** (Use this section if your agents have been trained in LAMA for call path control)
Make a check (√) if LAMA is complete or a slash (/) if not.

○ ○ ○ ○ ○ ○ ○ ○

○ ○ ○ ○ ○ ○ ○ ○

## Acknowledgements:
Find three things to praise on this call.  Be specific

_____

_____

_____

## Challenges/Self Correction/Plan
List challenges and the plan to improve.

1. What is the challenge? _____

2. What will be different? _____

3. How will you remember to be different? _____

4. When will it be done? _____

## Challenges/ Self Correction/Plan
1. _____

2. _____

3. _____

4. _____

Printed in the United States
71193LV00003B/238